MARKETING: THEORY AND PRACTICE

MACMILLAN STUDIES IN MARKETING MANAGEMENT

General Editor: Professor Michael J. Baker
University of Strathclyde

This series is designed to fill the need for a compact treatment of major aspects of marketing management and practice based essentially upon European institutions and experience. This is not to suggest that experience and practice in other advanced economies will be ignored, but rather that the treatment will reflect European custom and attitudes as opposed to American, which has tended to dominate so much of the marketing literature.

Each volume is the work of an acknowledged authority on that subject and combines a distillation of the best and most up-to-date research findings with a clear statement of their relevance to improved managerial practice. A concise style is followed throughout, and extensive use is made of summaries, check-lists and references to related work. Thus each work may be viewed as both an introduction to and a reference work on its particular subject. Further, while each book is self-contained, the series as a whole comprises a handbook of marketing management.

The series is designed for both students and practitioners of marketing. Lecturers will find the treatment adequate as the foundation for in-depth study of each topic by more advanced students who have already pursued an introductory and broadly based course in marketing. Similarly, managers will find each book to be both a useful *aide-mémoire* and a reference source.

The first titles in the series are:

International Marketing Management	J. M. Livingstone *University of Strathclyde*
Pricing	F. Livesey *UMIST*
Marketing: Theory and Practice	Professor Michael J. Baker (*editor*) *University of Strathclyde*
Product Policy and Management	Professor Michael J. Baker and Ronald McTavish *University of Strathclyde*

MARKETING
THEORY AND PRACTICE

edited by
Michael J. Baker

First published 1976 by
THE MACMILLAN PRESS LTD
London and Basingstoke
Associated companies in New York
Dublin Melbourne Johannesburg and Madras

ISBN 0 333 19820 4 (hard cover)
0 333 19821 2 (paper cover)

Printed in Great Britain by
THE ANCHOR PRESS LTD
Tiptree, Essex

Contents

PART 2 EVOLUTION OF MARKETING THOUGHT

PART 3 NEW DIRECTIONS IN MARKETING

Preface

The enigma of marketing is that it is one of man's oldest
activities and yet it is widely regarded as the most recent of
the business disciplines. In this book we examine some of the
reasons which seem to us to account for this apparent con-
tradiction as well as indicating why the theory and practice
of marketing must be integrated if the profession of marketing
is to achieve the status and credibility of professions such as
the law or medicine.

In fact many interesting parallels may be drawn between the
evolution and growth of these latter professions, especially
medicine and marketing. Like medicine, marketing has been
practised for thousands of years and has built up an enormous
wealth of descriptive information concerning the 'art'. Famili-
arity with this descriptive base has now become an essential
prerequisite, for it contains both the language or 'jargon'
which is a feature of any specialised activity as well as the
'case-law' which enables past experience to be applied to present
and future problems. However, as we note in Chapter 2, the
foundation of the modern profession of medicine is generally
agreed to have been laid with the transition from description
to analysis which accompanied Harvey's discovery of the
circulation of the blood. Since this discovery medicine has
borrowed extensively from other sciences in developing its own
theory and body of knowledge, but at the same time it has
recognised that the practice demands the establishment of a
relationship with the patient which mitigates direct translation
of theory into practice.

It is our view that if marketing is to progress it must achieve
a similar transition from art to applied science as has been
attained by medicine and that to do this it must establish a
sound theoretical foundation in its own right. Further, we
would argue that, in time, knowledge of this theoretical basis
should become an essential qualification for practice and that

those without it will become the 'quacks' of their profession. Much of this book constitutes an elaboration of this view.

In Part 1, 'The Foundations of Marketing', we trace the evolution of the marketing concept from its origins in barter to its modern statement as a managerial philosophy of business. Based on this historical review we next consider the need for theory in marketing as a preliminary to a survey of possible sources for such a theory. In Part 2, 'Evolution of Marketing Thought', we examine the theoretical foundations of four areas of central importance to the practice of marketing – consumer behaviour, communications, distribution and innovation. Of necessity such a review must be eclectic, but hopefully it will suffice to substantiate our claim as to the practical value of developing theory in marketing and will encourage the reader to extend his studies of the sources cited. Finally, in Part 3, 'New Directions in Marketing', we summarise current thinking on the application of marketing concepts and techniques beyond consumer-goods markets, with which it is traditionally associated, before concluding with a brief look at some of the sources of criticism of marketing.

Given the scope which we are attempting within such a small volume it will readily be appreciated that our efforts must represent a compromise between the breadth of coverage necessary to sustain our basic purpose of establishing the nature and relevance of marketing and the inextricable relationship between theory and practice, and the depth essential to raise the discussion above the trivial. To help reconcile these conflicting aims five authors have co-operated in developing material and their contributions are as follows:

Chapters 1, 7, 8 and 9   Michael J. Baker;
Chapters 2 and 3   Michael J. Baker and D. E. N. Dickson;
Chapter 4   Jennifer L. Drayton;
Chapter 5   Stephen T. Parkinson;
Chapter 6   A. J. Brown.

While each of these authors is responsible for his or her own contribution and any merit which the book possesses in whole or in part is to his or her personal credit, any deficiencies are the sole responsibility of the principal author.

Strathclyde University   Michael J. Baker
August 1975

List of Tables

List of Figures

Part I

The Foundations of Marketing

Chapter 1

Evolution of the Marketing Concept

INTRODUCTION

In this chapter we seek to provide some answers to the frequently posed question 'What is marketing?' We will argue that, essentially, marketing is concerned with exchange relationships between producers and users, suppliers and customers, and will suggest that uncertainty, confusion or misunderstanding as to the scope and nature of this exchange relationship would seem to stem from the fact that all of us have participated in such interchange and have formulated our own interpretation of its nature.

However, despite the multiplicity of definitions which are bound to arise from such a process, we propose that consensus is possible by distinguishing between marketing as a philosophy of exchange between persons and/or organisations and marketing as it has emerged as a business function. To establish this proposition we describe briefly the evolution of exchange from its early beginning in the form of barter to the sophisticated operation of a modern market economy. Against this background we identify the three managerial orientations which have characterised the development of the modern business organisation – production, sales and marketing – and argue that the recent development of a marketing orientation reflects a return to the original basis of exchange 'consumer sovereignty'.

Finally, some reference will be made to the relevance of a marketing orientation in the changing economic and social conditions which seem likely to obtain during the final quarter of the present century (a full discussion of this issue is undertaken in Part 3, 'New Directions in Marketing').

MARKETING = EXCHANGE

It is universally accepted that the lowest (and simplest) form of economic organisation is the subsistence economy in which each individual family unit is wholly dependent upon its own productive resources to satisfy its consumption needs. For our purposes it is unimportant to inquire into the precise social organisation of subsistence economies, for while this is of fundamental interest to the anthropologist, the distinction between gathering, hunting and/or pastoral nomadism is irrelevant in the absence of exchange, for, as Kotler has noted, 'it is a stage (of economic development) devoid of a concept of marketing'.[1]

Exchange first comes about where a producer creates a surplus in excess of the immediate needs of himself and his family, a surplus which he is willing to trade for some other good. Clearly, the potential for exchange is limited by the availability of other producers of different goods (or services) with surplus units which are intrinsically more attractive to the first producer than increased consumption of his own output (in the language of the economist they have a greater 'marginal utility'). In turn, the owners of these surpluses must seek supplies of the first producer's surplus. Assuming, therefore, that two producers of different products are brought into contact, each of whom has a desire for units of the other's surplus, it is logical to assume that any exchange effected by them is to their mutual satisfaction. In my opinion this is the essence of marketing – a mutually satisfying exchange relationship.

However, if we were to suggest this as our definition of marketing, that is 'Marketing is a process of exchange between individuals and/or organisations which is concluded to the mutual benefit and satisfaction of the parties', then clearly this proposition would go far beyond what most people consider to be the scope of the subject. In no small measure such rejection would arise from the modern interpretation of marketing as a business function which has evolved in its most extreme form in the sale of mass-consumption, packaged convenience products. As such it is appropriate to stress the point made in the preceding paragraph that the essence of an exchange relationship is freedom to decide how much of one's own surplus of any good or service, or title to any good or service, one is prepared to commute into supplies of some other good or service. Whether in fact this constitutes 'marketing' in the modern idiom can only be established by tracing the development of exchange relationships from their first beginnings in barter.

As a result of chance, application or natural aptitude most persons develop a particular skill in some aspect of life. If such skill yields an output of goods or services in demand by other persons, then the benefits of specialisation are immediately apparent. Increased productivity arising out of task specialisation results in a concomitant growth in the potential for exchange and this stage of economic development is generally associated with the genesis of the market-place. The need for an agreed meeting place where exchanges might be effected is obvious, for otherwise much productive time will be lost in seeking out potential customers for one's output who also possess supplies of desired goods or services. Similarly, as the degree of specialisation increases so does the assortment of goods, which further complicates the problem of bringing together two parties with a mutual interest in exchange.

To facilitate barter, at least two interrelated problems must be resolved – the problem of timing and the problem of value. Value is an essentially subjective concept and, like beauty, lies in the eye of the beholder. However, for an exchange to meet our criterion that it be 'mutually satisfying' it is clear that the parties to the exchange must agree on the basis for a subjective opinion as to 'value'. In formulating this value judgement the parties are bound to be guided by the more generalised value system evolved by the social grouping of which they are members. However, it would seem that there are certain concepts fundamental to most value systems amongst which may be numbered scarcity, utility and skill.

While scarcity may result from a natural deficiency, as is the case with precious metals, or from the time and effort required to create a unit of supply, physical scarcity in and of itself is insufficient to invest an object with value. Only if it is perceived as possessing utility in the widest sense of the word will people prize its ownership. Thus utility is inextricably linked with concepts of value, as it is with concepts of skill, that is the scarcity value of a skill is also proportionate to its perceived utility.

Given that one has developed generalised criteria for judging value, it is obvious that agreement on a unit of measurement will greatly facilitate comparative judgements on the exchange value of widely differing goods and services. Such a unit of measurement may take any form so long as it is universally recognised and accepted within the community which wishes to use it, and has been expressed in terms of cattle, shells, beads, and so forth, as well as its modern equivalent, money.

Evolution of a standard unit of exchange goes a long way to solving the problems of barter, for it provides a common denominator for estimating the value of goods and services as well as mitigating problems of timing. These latter are bound to arise as a result of disequilibrium between supply and demand, and, in the case of barter, are exacerbated by differences in the value and divisibility of different outputs. Universally acceptable units of exchange act as a store of value and so alleviate these timing problems.

Clearly the evolution of a money economy greatly encouraged increased specialisation and led to the development of sophisticated institutions for facilitating exchange both nationally and internationally. However, while increased specialisation led to enormous improvements in productivity in the manufacture of products, primary and tertiary activities – mining and farming – distribution and personal services were less amenable to improvement through specialisation and the division of labour.

Eventually the benefits of the division of labour were subject to diminishing returns in manufacturing industry too and the next step forward had to await the application of technology to the productive process. With the development of steam power an industrial revolution was set in train which enabled man's productive capacity to break through the plateau which it had reached when limited by natural power sources – wind and water – and the slow increase in population.

The history of the industrial revolution is familiar to us all and does not bear repetition here. Suffice it to say that increased productivity enabled a rapid increase in population which provided both the need for more sophisticated marketing institutions as well as the means of supplying them. However, it is important to recognise that while we speak of an industrial 'revolution' the actual process was more evolutionary and extended over a much longer period of time than is consistent with the connotations of revolution. Certainly there was no immediate solution to the grinding poverty which the working classes had endured since time immemorial, and the critical problem remained that of increasing the supply of the basic necessities of life. It was this emphasis which has led to the era being characterised as production orientated.

FROM PRODUCTION TO MARKETING ORIENTATION

Nowadays it is fashionable to distinguish different managerial approaches to the conduct of business and to suggest that there are fundamental differences between a production, a sales and a marketing operation.[2] The validity of such a proposition must of course depend upon how one defines a production, a sales and a marketing orientation, and it is necessary to put forward and examine such definitions before passing judgement.

As indicated in the preceding section the endemic problem of mankind was (and still is in many developing countries) a basic disequilibrium between supply and demand. In the face of such disequilibrium the concept of homeostasis predicates the action of natural forces to restore balance in the system. Clearly, the restoration of balance may arise or be brought about by either increasing supply, through increased productivity, or by reducing demand. In the nature of things man is a wanting animal and so seeks to increase supply, although in the case of warfare this is pursued in a negative manner more akin to demand reduction. Generally, however, demand reduction results from natural causes beyond man's immediate control, such as famine and disease, and history clearly demonstrates that population growth has been checked or declined when demand has caught up with or has overtaken available supply.

Because of the unpredictable incidence of the natural population controls of famine and disease, and recognising the need to increase the labour supply to maintain or improve production, most human societies have encouraged fertility. Indeed many religions contain a positive invocation to 'go forth and multiply' which has not been challenged seriously until very recent times. Thus, although Malthus warned in his *Essay on Population* that if the population continued to expand geometrically while production expanded in an arithmetic progression there would develop a major disequilibrium between supply and demand which could only be resolved by the natural controls, his warning fell into disrepute due to its failure to come into early effect. With the benefit of hindsight we can now see that supply did not expand arithmetically in the nineteenth century – it grew exponentially and more rapidly in the industrialised economies than did population, thus giving rise to a very significant improvement in the standards of living enjoyed by the members of those economies.

Today, however, there has been a Malthusian revival which has received perhaps its greatest support from the work of Jay Forrester[3] at the Massachusetts Institute of Technology (M.I.T.) and from the project sponsored by the Club of Rome which developed from this, preliminary reports of which are contained in *The Limits to Growth*.[4] The thesis underlying neo-Malthusianism is essentially that the world is a finite resource which will be rapidly exhausted if present consumption trends are allowed to continue, being reinforced by the multiplier effect of a rapidly expanding population.

In the medium term of three or four generations it is not too difficult to reject the pessimism of the Meadows model which predicts catastrophe long before this, by pointing out that Meadows, like Malthus, has fallen into the trap of extrapolating population and consumption geometrically and technological innovation and production arithmetically. However, for the longer term, even if one assumes that the means of sustaining life are available, it is clear that this planet can only physically accommodate a certain level of population. In recognition of this fact, as well as the validity of many of the arguments of the neo-Malthusians, the case for stabilising demand by population control is considered a much more viable and realistic solution to the human predicament than are attempts to increase supply. If, therefore, a production orientation is considered synonymous with efforts to increase supply, we can readily understand why it should have occupied a central place in the thinking of entrepreneurs from time immemorial. Further, given that the capacity to create over-supply only exists in a limited number of the world's economies it is not difficult to see why it should remain the focus of immediate effort in those countries with a supply deficiency *vis-à-vis* their present population.

King summarises the period of production orientation as 'an era of managerial concern with problems of capacity creation, work methods, and volume production'.[5] However, as he continues to point out, 'Although it is not suggested that corporate management gave no consideration during this period to the markets for which they produced, it appears that, generally, problems related to manufacturing assumed greater significance than did those related to identification and development of markets.'

While King is confining his discussion to the twentieth century it is quite obvious, for the reasons discussed above, that his comments are equally applicable to preceding centuries. It seems to me, therefore, that we render entrepreneurs a grave disservice if we use 'production orientated' in a pejorative sense and with overtones which imply that such an orientation ignores consumer needs. Rather, it seems to me that the production-orientated manager got his priorities right, in that demand for basic goods and services was clearly identifiable and that an emphasis upon volume rather than differentiation or choice was eminently sensible in that it went a long way towards maximising total satisfaction. Certainly, by achieving the economies of mass production, Henry Ford made his model-T available to vast segments of the population who otherwise would never have had the opportunity to own the basic product – a car – which they sought, the colour of which was essentially irrelevant. Yet today we cite 'You can have any colour of car as long as it's black' as the antithesis of marketing – a view that it is difficult if not impossible to sustain if one adopts the definition proposed earlier that marketing is concerned with mutually satisfying exchange relationships. As better than 60 per cent of American car sales in 1920 were Fords, we must accept that two-thirds of American car buyers felt this to be a more satisfying situation than buying (or not being able to afford to buy) the products of the myriad producers who collectively accounted for the remaining third of the market.

The situation which was to bring the production orientation into disrepute was what I have referred to elsewhere as 'the creation of "excess" supply'.[6] Excess supply is of course a comparative state and applies only to certain categories of products under very limited conditions, foremost amongst which is a presumption of available discretionary consumer purchasing power that is only satisfied, and then only partially, in the most affluent societies. However, from the firm's point of view, a state of excess supply begins to become apparent when the market ceases to absorb all of its output and exhibits price inelasticity of demand within the range which would be acceptable to the firm, that is to stimulate increased consumption, it would be necessary to sell at an unacceptably low price.

Faced with price inelasticity of demand for its output, and a situation in which the joint potential supply of the firm and its immediate competitors exceeds effective demand, managements' immediate reaction tends to be to maintain volume through non-price competition and especially by means of product differentiation, promotion and selling effort.

In the short term it is easiest to increase the sales effort, and for this reason there was a transitional period which King identifies as the sales-management orientation between the production-management orientation and the present emphasis upon marketing. Simplistically, the sales-management orientatation, which prevailed between 1930 and 1950 in the United States, may be characterised as 'selling what we can make' in contradistinction to 'making what we can sell' which is considered a central feature of the marketing concept. However, these catch phrases do scant justice to the philosophical difference between a sales-management and marketing approach.

From the sales manager's standpoint, products and services are given and potential customers must be persuaded to see them as the solution to a generalised consumption need. From the marketer's standpoint customers are given and potential products must be developed or modified to match specific consumption needs. Thus, where the production- or sales-orientated manager would tend to ask himself 'What do customers want?', the marketer would ask the customers themselves and then proceed to organise a supply of the desired objects.

One of the first firms to embrace a marketing approach was the American General Electric Company, and King cites two quotations which help spell out this fundamental difference between selling and marketing:

Under the traditional 'sales' concept, engineering designed a product, manufacturing produced it – and then the sales people were expected to sell it. Under the modern 'marketing' concept, the whole business process starts with marketing research and sales forecasting to provide a sound, factual customer-oriented basis for planning all business operations, and the business function which has sales responsibility now participates in all the stages of the business planning process.[7]

[the marketing concept] introduces the marketing man at the beginning rather than the end of the production cycle and would integrate marketing into each phase of the business. Thus marketing, through its studies and research, will establish for the engineer, the designer and the manufacturing man what the customer wants in a given product, what price he is willing to pay, and where and when it will be wanted. Marketing would have authority in product planning, production scheduling and inventory control, as well as in the sales, distribution and servicing of the product.[8]

Similarly, Robert J. Keith's description of the role of marketing in the Pillsbury Company serves to reinforce this point:

Marketing is viewed in our company today as the function which plans and executes the sale – all the way from the inception of the idea, through its development and execution, to the sale to the customer. Marketing begins and ends with the consumer. The idea for a new product is conceived after careful study of her wants and needs, her likes and dislikes. With the idea in hand, the marketing department functions as a universal joint in the corporation, marshalling all the forces of the corporation to translate the idea into product and the product into sales.[9]

FULL CIRCLE

In describing the evolution of the marketing concept it appears that we have been guilty of considerable arrogance in presuming it to be of recent origin. In reality it seems to me that if our early definition of marketing as 'a process of exchange between individuals and/or organisations which is concluded to the mutual benefit and satisfaction of the parties' is acceptable, then marketing is as old as exchange relationships themselves. However, as society has developed, and has harnessed the power of science and technology to assist it in meeting the apparently insatiable demand for goods and services, so it has been necessary to evolve new institutions and new mechanisms to cope with the complexity which has accompanied this development.

It follows that if the criterion to be used to judge or measure the effectiveness of a single exchange relationship is the mutual satisfaction derived from it, then, in the aggregate, marketing (exchange?) will be at its most efficient when it maximises aggregate satisfaction. If this is so, then, as we have already argued, the much despised production orientation with its emphasis upon manufacturing and volume of output may be the most appropriate to conditions of chronic under-supply. Under such conditions the nature of demand is likely to be as self-evident to the entrepreneur responsible for setting up and controlling a factory with an output measured in millions of identical units as it was and is to the supplier who engaged in a direct one-to-one relationship with his customer.

Thus it would seem more accurate to speak not of the emergence of the marketing concept in the 1950s but rather to talk about the need to reappraise the precise nature of consumer demand due to the changes brought about by the physical separation of producer and customer (accompanied by the potential to create excess supply in some sectors of production) in order to ensure that we maximise aggregate satisfaction. Asking customers what they want can hardly be as revolutionary a step as some writers would have us believe! More likely it reflects the basic and continuing nature of exchange, that is consumer sovereignty.

MARKETING – PHILOSOPHY OR FUNCTION?

Unfortunately, while the philosophy of marketing is firmly rooted in the principle of consumer sovereignty, even if only out of enlightened self-interest, there is a growing body of criticism which believes and argues to the contrary. It would be naive to deny that this criticism has foundation for there are sufficient well-established examples[10] to warrant a case against modern marketing practices. However, to establish that some members of a community are criminals is not to prove that all are. Similarly, to identify some misleading advertisements or malpractices such as pyramid selling (albeit that the latter only thrives on the greed of the victims who want something for nothing) is not to substantiate a case that marketing as a whole is against the consumer interest.

Further, it seems to me that most criticism is directed at the practice, or perhaps it would be nearer the truth to say the malpractice, of marketing and not against the philosophy or principles as we have outlined them above. Indeed, given our definition of marketing it is difficult to see how anyone could ever take exception to it. On the other hand, it is not difficult to understand how ordinary consumers can become dubious about marketing when they have no clear definition of what the marketing concept is supposed to be, save possibly a cliché such as 'the customer is always right', and so can only judge from their own direct experience at the hands of marketers.

However, while one is forced to acknowledge defects in the function of marketing arising from certain marketing practices, it would be unwise to accept all of the criticism directed against it by consumerists. Because consumerists are intelligent, articulate and often highly vocal one should not automatically assume that they have a monopoly of the truth nor that one must accept their point of view. Accordingly, while most advertisers, and certainly all responsible ones, would agree with the desirability of truth in advertising, this is not to concede that all advertising should be purely factual and devoid of any subjective associations or connotations.

Where the consumerists go wrong in their condemnation of marketing is in their insistence upon a concept of objective rationality the origin of which would seem to be a simplifying assumption necessary to make early price theory work. As economics has become more sophisticated it has become possible to relax such rigid assumptions as homogeneity of demand and supply and to admit, as Lawrence Abbott[11] has pointed out, that 'What people really desire are not products but satisfying experiences.' Thus, as Abbott comments,

> what is considered satisfying is a matter for individual decision: it varies according to one's tastes, standards, beliefs and objectives – and these vary greatly, depending on individual personality and cultural environment. Here is a foundation for a theory of choice broad enough to embrace Asiatic as well as Eastern cultures, nonconformists as well as slaves to convention, Epicureans, stoics, cynics, roisterers, religious fanatics, dullards, and intellectual giants alike.

In fact, a theory of choice founded on consumer sovereignty.

To criticise 'Admass' (mass advertising) for treating all consumers as the same, and mindless automatons to boot, would seem contradictory to say the least when reinforced by an all-embracing demand that we all buy on the basis of price and product specification while ignoring all aesthetic and/or subjective associations.

But merely to deny the consumerists' case against marketing is insufficient. Rather it is necessary to show that marketing too possesses a theoretical foundation which, without claiming it to be a better theory than any other theory of how people behave, at least deserves equal consideration. Only if marketers can raise the argument above the trivial of the rights and wrongs of specific marketing actions does it seem to me that we may be able to persuade our critics that marketing is a subject worthy of serious study, and an honourable profession as well. Further, I believe that it is essential to establish that marketing is not merely another transitional phase, like the sales-management orientation of the 1930s and 1940s, to be characterised as one of 'demand stimulation' and 'conspicuous consumption' and wholly inappropriate to the growing awareness of the need to conserve our limited resources, but a social philosophy of increasing relevance.

To this end, in the next two chapters we examine the need for a theory of marketing, and its likely nature and sources before considering how theory may improve our understanding of specific areas such as marketing communications and distribution. Finally, we broaden our review once again to discuss the role marketing has to play in the changing social and economic conditions likely to obtain in the final quarter of the century.

Chapter 2

The Need for Theory in Marketing

INTRODUCTION

The purpose of this chapter is to establish why it is considered essential that the study and practice of marketing should be founded upon a sound theoretical base.

To do this one must first specify what one means by 'theory' and then identify its role. Equipped with a definition of theory we may then enquire into its nature, which in turn will allow us to focus attention upon its function. This consideration suggests that theory is essential to the development of an integrated body of knowledge and raises the question as to how theory evolves or is developed.

A basic distinction is frequently drawn between 'art' and 'science' and we review what appears to us to be the difference between the two prior to a fuller consideration of the nature of science and the scientific method in the context of its possible relevance to marketing.

THE DEFINITION OF THEORY

The word 'theory' is normally associated in people's minds with the development of ideas or conjectures about the manner or ways in which part of the world works. From the Oxford dictionary we find that one derivation of theory is from the Greek *oewpia* which was used in the sense of 'pertaining to or connected with public spectacles, religious functions and solemn embassies', which we presume were looked at by spectators as an attempt on the part of actors or participants to interpret one way of looking at part of the real world. With the passage of time the meaning of theory became more generalised and the Latin root *theoria* was used to mean 'a looking at or a speculation or a contemplation'. Today however, we have endowed the word 'theory' with a more specific meaning and for our purposes will adopt the working definition suggested in the Oxford dictionary which defines a theory as being 'a scheme or system of ideas or statements held as an explanation of a group of facts or phenomena'.

THE NATURE OF THEORY

A review of human progress would seem to suggest that the main catalyst is a change in emphasis in the orientation of critical thought from a 'descriptive' basis to a basis which may be defined as primarily 'analytical'. For example, in the field of medicine early developments were confined to general descriptions of the human body and the naming of its various parts. In turn this descriptive base permitted the transference of ideas concerning the nature and causes of disease from one case to another. However, with Harvey's discovery of the circulation of the blood the orientation of medicine changed from being one of description to one of analysis based upon a theory which satisfies the definition advanced earlier.

Just as Harvey's discovery provided the foundation for the modern profession of medicine so too have similar breakthroughs provided the basis for the development and extension of other fields of human endeavour. At the same time it must be recognised that many breakthroughs in thought and practice have occurred without the application of developed theory. Thus most early innovations were developed by inventors whose approach could be defined as pragmatic, as was the case when James Watt designed the first rudimentary steam-engine based upon his observations of the pressure exerted upon the lid of a kettle as a result of the build up of steam which took place when it boiled upon an open fire. The thermo-dynamic theory of heat transfer had not been developed yet steam-engines were constructed and worked successfully for over a century before this theory was evolved. But, with the development of a theory of thermo-dynamics the design of the steam-engine underwent a revolutionary change, and from that time onwards they were designed largely according to theoretical principles rather than by studying and applying empirical data concerning the past design and operation of steam-engines. As a result of this application of theory the efficiency of the steam-engine increased geometrically by contrast with the arithmetic rate of progress which had characterised it prior to a statement of theory concerning its operation.

This same process of development from applied art to analytical or theoretical knowledge has held good in many fields of human activity. When these activities first developed they were essentially based upon the application of skill or technique and characterised as 'arts'. However, with the formulation and statement of a sound theoretical base a whole new insight into the activity began to emerge and the transition took place from art to science.

However, before going on to consider the nature of the differences between art and science it will be helpful if we delineate three basic requirements which any theorist must satisfy.

A basic requirement of any theory are definitions which state clearly the meaning of the various terms which will be used in that theory. The need for clear and precise definitions is obvious, for without them we will be uncertain as to what constitutes a relevant observation and how to interpret it in order to test the theory. In addition to defining the terms which are to be used, an area of science frequently termed 'semantics', the statement of an adequate theory also requires that we define the conditions or assumptions under which the theory will hold. The third requirement of a theory is that it should be built upon hypotheses about the way in which things actually behave or about relationships between things in the real world. In essence hypotheses are working guesses to which we attach a high antecedent probability that they will be validated by the collection and analysis of evidence or data. Thus a hypothesis differs from a theory in that it has not been demonstrated to yield predictions with an accuracy greater than that which could be achieved if predictions were made by some random device. However, once a hypothesis has been shown to be able to yield predictions with greater accuracy than would arise from such a random process, then we will term it a 'theory'. In turn, if a theory can be demonstrated to yield perfectly accurate predictions every time it is used, then that theory will take on the status of a 'law'.

The usefulness and quality of marketing theory will depend upon the way in which definitions, assumptions and hypotheses are combined together. The theory or model which is produced may be regarded as a simplification of a part of reality which usually fits the observed facts approximately rather than exactly. Thus the role of a researcher in any field is to try and impose order upon the observations he makes of that part of the real world which is his area of interest, for otherwise these observations will be little more than a confused jumble of facts and ideas. The statement of a theory demands that these facts and ideas should be brought together in a related and meaningful way. Thus in many respects a valid theory is very similar to a road map. A valid theory, like a valid road map, requires to be based on facts if it is to be realistic and useful. If it is too detailed and incorporates every hedge and post upon the road it will be confusing and of little use to the driver using it as a means of getting from one place to another. On the other hand, if it is insufficiently detailed, it will be inadequate as a guide to real-life situations.

To be useful, then, a theory, like a road map, must satisfy certain functions, functions which to some degree are dependent upon the structure of the theory itself. Until now, researchers in the field of marketing have tended to limit the functions of theory to those of description and prescription, that is the ability to give direction. These two functions are basic to all theory but in addition there are others which should be performed by any theory with pretensions to adequacy, namely the functions of delimitation, generation and integration.

Delimitation Function

While the basic function of any theory is to describe part of reality such description must operate selectively. This selection is the delimiting function and means in effect that the theory cannot include everything in the world of reality. Thus a theory which does not delimit in this fashion would break under its own excess of explanation. The process of deciding what to include and exclude from a theory through this process of delimitation depends very much upon the purpose for which the theory is being constructed.

The Generative Function

The generative function may be defined as the capacity to create testable hypotheses and encompasses the processes which we otherwise describe as theoretical speculation, creativity, or even 'hunch'. Thus as well as being founded upon tested hypotheses a theory must also generate new hypotheses which will permit us to extend our understanding and knowledge.

When a theory is used to stimulate empirical investigation it is spoken of as using the theory 'heuristically'. The heuristic use of theory is often made by analogy, for example Freud used the physical concepts of hydraulic fluid to express mental states.

The Integrative Function

This function of theory refers to the ability to bring together the various constructs and propositions which have been elucidated by the researcher into a more or less consistent and useful whole. Thus the objective of theorists working in an area such as marketing must be to endeavour to integrate and pull together their ideas into a coherent and interdependent unit which warrants identification as a formal theory.

However, such a process of formalisation can have side-effects such as confusion and inconsistency. For example, in the field of marketing a number of independent researchers have attempted to construct complex theories of consumer behaviour in order to explain the buying process. As Jennifer L. Drayton points out in her discussion of these theories in Chapter 4, these theories contradict as much as confirm one another.

The integrative function is of prime importance in the development of theory. In many ways marketing like psychology has been going through a period in which the emphasis has been upon a number of micro or miniature theories which constitute an adequate explanation of some part or parts of the subject (the 'piecemeal' approach). Thus some observers such as MacInnes are of the opinion that the first priority in developing theory in marketing must be the integration of these various pieces of emerging theory into a consistent whole (a 'holistic' approach).

THE NEED FOR A THEORY IN MARKETING

As we indicated in the first chapter the practice of marketing has existed since the first exchange relationship. However, in tracing the evolution of marketing from the early days of barter through to the statement of the modern marketing concept in the early 1950s, it became apparent that the need for a formal restatement of the basis upon which such relationships exist arose out of the separation which had occurred between buyer and seller. In turn the degree and extent of this separation reflects the development of a very complex and sophisticated system for matching highly specific wants with supplies of goods and services capable of satisfying these wants.

In recent years it has been fashionable to decry the operation of the marketing system and to give great attention to its deficiencies rather than to its achievements. In large degree it is felt that many of the deficiencies which exist in the marketing system arise out of a lack of understanding as to its actual operation. It is recognition and acceptance of the need to improve our understanding of the manner in which the system works which underlies the need to develop a workable theory of exchange. It must be stressed that the key word in the preceding sentence is 'workable' for clearly there are well-developed theories of exchange in economics and in the behavioural sciences. However, from our point of view these are inadequate for they are an oversimplified and stylised representation of real-world behaviour. Further, it is our opinion that a theory of marketing demands a synthesising of concepts from both the economic and the behavioural sciences if it is to constitute an adequate explanation of the true nature of exchange.

In many senses the practice of marketing today is in a very similar situation to that which obtained prior to the statement of the law of thermo-dynamics in terms of the development of the steam-engine. Thus, as Halbert has pointed out,[1] marketing needs to develop a theory both to improve operational performance as well as to satisfy an intellectual desire to evolve an explanation of a confused world. With the formulation and statement of a theory of marketing we could look forward to the more effective solution of immediate operating problems and so could concentrate our attention on the more important and basic problems which underlie them. Further, increased operational efficiency would also free practitioners from 'fire-fighting' activities and so leave them with more time in which to solve these problems. Thus the increasing complexity of business makes the need for theory even more pressing than hitherto in order to speed up and improve our decision-making capability. At the same time it appears that developments in other sciences have created the intellectual and analytical tools necessary to the statement of a theory of marketing.

MARKETING AND THE SCIENTIFIC METHOD

At a number of places in the preceding pages we have referred to science and scientific method and it is appropriate that we should now consider the relevance that these may have for the formulation of a theory of marketing.

As hinted earlier, the factor which tends to differentiate science from art or applied skill is that science goes beyond mere description and seeks to provide an explanation of why things are what they are. Thus one of the main objectives of science has been that of spelling out the interrelationship between the parts of the structure in order to derive laws or principles which may serve as a basis for prediction, decision and action. Prediction in any field of study is possible only to the extent that uniformity exists in the phenomena under study. Indeed it is probably because the conditions and events of a physical nature are found to have a relatively higher degree of uniformity that predictions regarding them can be thought of as comparatively reliable with the result that the methods by which such phenomena have been studied have become the standards for scientific research and the basis of what has been termed 'the scientific method'.

In an article entitled 'Is Marketing a Science?' Robert D. Buzzell[2] suggests that a science is 'a classified and systemized body of knowledge . . . organised around one or more central theories and a number of general principles . . . usually expressed in quantitative terms . . . knowledge which permits the prediction and, under some circumstances the control of future events'. Invariably science which conforms to this definition is the outcome of a process known as 'the scientific method' which is usually recognised as possessing a number of clearly defined steps: (1) observation and measurement; (2) experimentation; (3) classification; and (4) accurate generalisation.

While we have suggested that the basic distinction between art and science rests on the fact that the latter goes beyond description to explanation, none the less it is clear that the first step in the scientific method must be the collection and description of facts. Based upon observation the first distinction which a person is likely to make is qualitative, for example A is bigger than B and A is bigger than C. It is immediately apparent that such qualitative statements severely limit our ability to make inferences about the relationship between B and C. For this reason science lays great emphasis upon precise measurement and quantification and so enables us to make much more accurate and elaborate statements about the relationship between objects.

If we assume that the first step in the evolution of scientific methods is the chance or random observation of objects and events, then it is clear that our knowledge and understanding will be greatly improved if these observations are undertaken in a systematic manner. Even greater progress becomes possible when such systematic observation is complemented by experimentation. Experiments may be conceived of and undertaken for a variety of reasons but all rest upon the principle that every natural event is a consequence of preceding and ascertainable conditions of its physical environment. It follows, therefore, that if one changes the conditions in the physical environment then one will produce corresponding changes in the event. Amongst the various types of experiment may be distinguished exploratory investigations in which one varies inputs in a controlled manner in order to determine the effect upon the outputs; experiments to test accepted principles, for example Gallileo's experiments with weights whereby he disproved the Aristotelian law that material bodies fall with velocities proportional to their weights; experiments to check on chance observations; and experiments to test hypotheses.

Clearly, experimentation results in a great improvement in both the quantity and quality of data available to scientists. However, to be meaningful this data must now be classified as a basis for analysis and a statement of accurate generalisations. This process whereby one develops generalisations from particular instances and events is known as 'induction' and, irrespective of the name given to them, all models, principles, laws and theories possess the common property that they are generalisations about an area of reality arrived at by the process of abstracting from reality

Good representations of phenomena abstracted from reality can also be used to explain occurrences or even to make predictions. This method is known as 'deduction' – a process of reasoning from general assumptions or statements to particular conclusions. It is clear that deductive methods permit the verification of conclusions arrived at by inductive reasoning, and thus the cycle of induction, deduction and verification constitutes the framework of the scientific method.

The need for a scientific approach to the solution of marketing problems was well exemplified in a paper delivered by Colin McDonald at the Market Research Society's Seminar on Strategic Advertising Decisions in November 1974.[3] Given the magnitude of advertising expenditures (£874 million in 1973 in the United Kingdom alone) it is not surprising that marketers have long sought for some measure of the return on this outlay but, so far, with a singular lack or success. In McDonald's view this lack of success is due to speculative theorising which fails to observe the rules of the scientific method, and especially its failure first to observe and describe the phenomenon. Thus he comments:

> I find myself very much in agreement with David Berdy[4] when he categorises most of the approaches to advertising as ideological, or fundamentalist, and for that reason sterile, and complains of its failure to adopt a true scientific approach in spite of trying: Outside the pure sciences . . . there is an inverse relationship between preoccupation with theoretical structures and the understanding of practical techniques or processes. You cannot observe a theory without observing facts; such short cuts are a negation of the scientific method.

In deciding just what one should observe, McDonald cites three basic questions posed by advertisers:
(1) How should we decide the size of the advertising appropriation?
(2) How should we decide the media mix?
(3) How should we decide whether to have continuous or burst advertising?
He goes on to say that 'The second and third of these questions are subsidiary to the first one. The first question involves *what* advertising is trying to do (objectives) and how we measure that it is doing it; the other two questions are about how to achieve what is determined by the first.'

But, after reviewing the advertisers' viewpoint, McDonald is forced to conclude that an approach based upon measuring advertising's success (or lack of it) in achieving predetermined objectives is doomed to failure. As he trenchantly points out, 'The trouble is that, *because* there is ignorance of advertising effect, people have no basis on which to *set* objectives in the first place. Thus the objectives they do set (when indeed they propose any) tend to be circular; they reflect their existing preconceptions.' Accordingly, it follows that one must first observe, record and measure what actually happens as a result of advertising in terms of perception, awareness, attitude and behavioural change. In turn, as we are concerned with people, we must study them as individuals and over time, which militates against the type of aggregate and cross-sectional studies which have predominated in the past.

Once we have built up a sound base of observations, McDonald feels that we should not be so constrained by the true scientific method as to become heavily involved in experimentation. This opinion is predicated on the belief that the high level of interdependence between many marketing variables (for example distribution and promotion) makes it very difficult to separate out their effects and that attempts to do so may be sterile and self-defeating (as they often have been in the past). Thus experimentation should be used where feasible and appropriate but should not be regarded as a *sine qua non* of progression to the stages of classification and generalisation

Throughout his paper McDonald returns again and again to the need for a sound empirical basis to theory founded upon observation and testing of these observations, for otherwise there is a considerable danger of falling into the trap of circular reasoning. As an example of this he cites the DAGMAR model which is postulated on a premise that this is how advertising 'should' work and validated by data or evidence which proves the point – in other words a self-fulfilling prophecy.

THE DEVELOPMENT OF MARKETING THEORY

Much of what McDonald has to say about the measurement of advertising effectiveness would seem to be equally true of many other areas of marketing. Perhaps marketers lack sufficient humility to get back to first principles and collect raw data as the basis for developing their own theory, or perhaps we place too much reliance upon the theories which we have borrowed from other disciplines without validating them. Whatever the reason we are inclined to subscribe to the general view that while marketing is not yet worthy of the title 'science', there is no reason why it should not become so. However, to achieve scientific status we must accept the rigour implicit in the scientific method and begin at the beginning with observation and measurement and not jump into experimentation, classification and generalisation without this essential foundation

Assuming then that we accept the desirability of committing effort and resources to the development of marketing theory, and are prepared to adopt a scientific approach, what criteria should we seek to satisfy? On this issue we can do no better than reproduce Leslie Rodger's statement of the requirements of good theory.[5]

(i) it must provide the means of classifying, organising, and integrating information relevant to the factual world of business;
(ii) it must provide a technique of thinking about marketing problems, and a perspective for practical action;
(iii) it must make available an analytical tool-kit to be drawn on as appropriate in the solution of marketing problems;
(iv) it should provide a basis for the explanation, prediction, and perhaps even the control of marketing processes and events;
(v) it should, in time, permit the derivation of a number of principles, possibly even laws, of marketing behaviour.

If we adopt these criteria then it is apparent that there are at least some ideas and concepts which enjoy currency among both academics and practitioners that go a long way towards satisfying them. Thus, while this chapter has been concerned primarily with establishing the need for theory and the benefits of a scientific approach to its formulation, in the process of which we have been critical of non-scientific methods, this is not to say that marketing lacks any theoretical foundations at all. In fact the development of marketing thought may be traced back to at least the beginnings of the present century, and in the next chapter we review some of its more important sources.

Chapter 3
The Sources of Marketing Theory

INTRODUCTION

In the preceding chapter we were concerned primarily with defining the nature and function of theory in order to justify our view that a theoretical foundation is essential to the development of any body of knowledge. Further, we endeavoured to show that improvement in practice is dependent upon the development of such a body of knowledge which, in turn, would seem to proceed most effectively when based upon a scientific approach. In this chapter we turn our attention to an examination of the progress made towards the evolution of theory in marketing.

Our examination of the present state of marketing theory commences with a review of the proposition that we must draw upon concepts and hypotheses developed in other disciplines, notably the social sciences, as the basis for such theory. Accordingly we consider 'borrowing' on three levels – content, techniques and concepts. This survey leads naturally to a discussion of the way in which different facts or other evidence may be combined into a distinctive or coherent body of knowledge and to a brief synopsis of the development of marketing thought along the lines proposed by Bartels. Finally, we examine specific sources of marketing theory, such as economics and the behavioural sciences, as a preliminary to the detailed analysis of the particular marketing topics which comprise Part 2 of this book.

BASIC SOURCES

In his seminal contribution *The Meaning and Sources of Marketing Theory*, Michael Halbert makes the point early on that 'marketing, however, has no recognised central theoretical basis such as exists for any other disciplines, notably the physical sciences and, in some cases, the behavioural sciences'.[1] At first glance the absence of such a recognised theoretical core seems somewhat surprising, particularly if one accepts that theory usually develops out of practice and that marketing has been practised ever since the first exchange relationship was entered into. However, as we noted in the previous chapter, the development of a theory usually results from a coalescing of two parallel forces, a practical desire to improve operational performance and an intellectual desire to evolve an explanation of a confused world. But, as a review of the evolution of the modern marketing management concept out of the production- and sales-management orientations which preceded it makes clear, in conditions of chronic under-supply improvement of operational performance demands that, before anything else, we must satisfy first-order needs which in turn places a premium upon increased productivity and output. Similarly, the intellectual desire to evolve an explanation of a confused world would tend to reflect this reality, which is why the problem of maximising the satisfaction to be derived from the consumption of scarce resources is central to economic theory

If one believes in the 'needs hierarchy' such as that proposed by Maslow, that is (1) physiological needs, (2) safety needs, (3) love needs, (4) esteem needs, and (5) the need for self-actualisation, in which each higher order of need only emerges when all needs on the preceding and lower levels have been satisfied, one can readily understand why the social sciences are of relatively recent origin. In a situation where virtually all needs are concentrated at the lowest physiological level we may anticipate that patterns of behaviour will be relatively simple and focused upon the acquisition of basic food, shelter and clothing. Only when these basic needs are satisfied and we move up the hierarchy does the intrinsic complexity of human behaviour become sufficiently marked to warrant investigation and explanation. Thus we can speculate that the development of conditions in which supply caught up with and sometimes exceeded demand, conditions which were to give rise to the function of marketing as we know it today, also created the conditions which favoured the development of the behavioural sciences.

It is our belief that any theory of marketing must be synthetic, in the sense that it must combine major concepts and ideas from both economics and the behavioural sciences. Although there is now a trend for each of these disciplines to consider the findings and theories of the other and to attempt to incorporate them in their own theories, the earlier development of both these disciplines has shown a marked neglect of the other. Thus, as we argue later, the theory of buyer behaviour based solely upon concepts of economic rationality, or alternatively one based upon behavioural concepts which ignore economic constraints upon behaviour, is unlikely to prove a satisfactory explanation of the way in which people behave in the real world. It is possible, therefore, that the need for a theory of marketing arises from recognition of the enormous complexity associated with exchange relationships and recognises that neither economics nor the behavioural sciences fully satisfies this need. If this is the case then it is not difficult to understand why progress towards a theory of marketing must of necessity be both painful and slow.

'BORROWING' AS A BASIS FOR MARKETING THEORY

Halbert suggests that if we are seeking a basis for marketing theory then we should be prepared to borrow from other fields. This we may do at three different levels of generality – content, techniques and concepts. When we are dealing with content we are concerned with the question of 'what' to study, that is with facts or data; when we are concerned with techniques we will be studying 'how' to apply certain methods to the generation of the content material; and when we are concerned with concepts, we will be referring, or endeavouring to refer, to 'why' the phenomena take place.

Content refers to the most specific class of material since it is concerned with observations, measurements and descriptions of the phenomena which are to be studied; thus content concerns facts or data from which a theory may be abstracted.

In Halbert's words, techniques are 'ways of generalising the content material' and so include techniques of research investigation and analysis. It is in this area that the most active and effective borrowing has taken place, and applied to marketing. Techniques include the processes of both measurement and analysis. From mathematics we borrow techniques like 'multiple regression' while from psychology we are liable to borrow the 'intelligence test' and the 'questionnaire', and from statistics analytical techniques which allow us to estimate percentages of a population likely to possess, or not possess, given characteristics based upon samples of that population.

In his search for appropriate techniques which may be applied to marketing, Halbert looks to the behavioural sciences, the business disciplines and the methodological sciences. He suggests that while few of the techniques developed and in common use are already well integrated into marketing many are beginning to exert considerable interest at the fringe of research.

However, borrowed and adapted techniques, no matter how powerful and useful they may be in their own area, offer no easy solution to marketing problems. Some of the most enthusiastic advocates of the management sciences have suggested that some of their techniques such as, for example, linear programming and operations research provide the means whereby many marketing problems could be solved more realistically. At best, however, these techniques probably offer us an additional analytical device the value of which depends very much upon the skill of the marketing analyst and upon the clarity with which problems can be stated and analysed when first identified.

While the borrowing of content and techniques often goes a long way toward the objective of improving operational performance, it is to concepts which we must look to provide the intellectual and explanatory aspects of theory. For, as Halbert notes, it is *'concepts, theories,* and *generalised ideas* that form the abstract but essential element that distinguishes a science from an art of practice'. As can be seen from Table 3.1, re-

TABLE 3.1

Contributions of various sciences and disciplines to a science of marketing

Science or discipline	Type of contribution		
	Content	Technique	Concept
Marketing	Major	Minor	
Business disciplines	Major	Minor	
Behavioural sciences	Minor	Major	Minor
Methodological sciences		Minor	Major

produced from Halbert, marketing has been least successful in borrowing concepts, and, according to Halbert, has developed no concepts of its own.

CONTRIBUTIONS TO A THEORY OF MARKETING

The increase in knowledge of most marketing specialists has come about as a result of utilising descriptive material, techniques and concepts from different fields of knowledge. As can be seen from Table 3.1, marketing has drawn from many different source areas, and these borrowings have often been so numerous and extensive that one can be forgiven for wondering whether they can be ever welded together into a coherent whole warranting recognition as a general theory of marketing.

This doubt is well founded, for most marketers have come into the subject from other disciplines and their view of it is imbued with concepts and ideas appropriate to this original discipline. Thus economists regard marketing as being primarily an area of applied economics and think about the subject in a very different way from behaviourists and management scientists.

In an article entitled 'The General Theory of Marketing'[2] Robert Bartels suggests that, just as in other areas of scientific and behavioural knowledge the subject area has moved through the process of development of practical ability to theoretical knowledge, so in marketing we may be already witnessing a similar move towards the development of a cohesive theory. In fact he argues that the very proliferation of facts may be forcing an integration of knowledge on a higher plane of unification and abstraction.

Bartels continues to argue that growth of theory in the marketing area may be thought of as analogous to the growth of a pile of sand or sand-castle which one builds on the beach when on holiday; the higher the sand-castle has to be, then the broader must be its base; the broader its base, the higher it must be built before a sharp peak or focus is obtained. The process of abstraction applied to the field of marketing may indeed be similar to this in its nature. If we are to give any credence to this point of view then a given base of fact supports its own structure of generalisation and abstraction as indicated in Figure 3.1(a). Further study may reinforce the theory which has already been devised through broadening the basis of enquiry. This has two effects upon the structure of thought. It may either, as a result of more and more empirical observations, raise the level of generalisation which can be based upon the myriad of facts, as for example is shown in Figure 3.1(*b*), or it may provide certain theories with relevant concepts and techniques which may or may not be capable of being unified into a more general theory, as is indicated in Figure 3.1(*c*). If there is any possibility of the

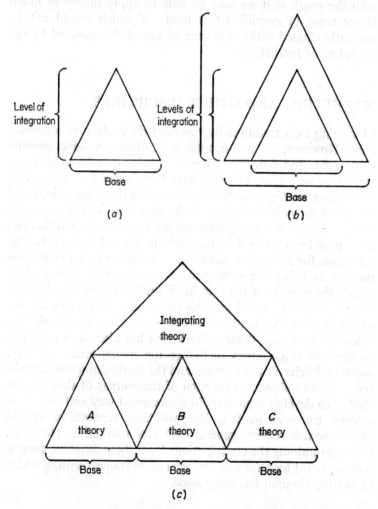

FIG. 3.1   *Levels of integration*

development of what could be called 'a general theory of marketing' then it will probably grow out of the approach suggested by Figures 3.1(*b*) or 3.1(*c*).

However, most observers are agreed that in its current state of development marketing still consists of a number of separate theories or piecemeal approaches which by and large fall into the pattern suggested by Figure 3.1(*c*). These separate theoretical areas may in time build up through a process of integration with the result that we may be able to apply theory to much larger areas of empirical fact many of which would not be currently classed within the area of knowledge covered by the discipline of marketing.

MARKETING AND OTHER DISCIPLINES

Marketing men traditionally regarded themselves as economic men. However, as non-economic motivations have become recognised, and different patterns of behaviour have been observed, so new areas of study have been opened to marketing. New views were not easily integrated with the assumptions and observations which represented the viewpoint of the economic man, but as we have suggested earlier the behaviourist theories have now been applied increasingly to the field of marketing. Alderson, for example, considered participants in the marketing process as being the same people whom sociologists studied within the context of the firm itself, and therefore he advanced a view that sociological theories had an important role to play in helping to understand marketing and to extend the basis provided by economic theory. Marketing has also drawn upon a number of other areas including the management sciences, social and behavioural sciences and the methodological sciences but, as noted above, so far each of these areas of thought has tended to develop separately in a piecemeal way and very little attempt has been made to integrate these separate areas and move towards a more general theory of marketing. However, before examining the contributions from these different areas it will be useful to trace the developmental stages through which marketing thought has progressed.

The Development of Marketing Thought

Probably the best-known chronicler of the history of marketing thought is Robert Bartels.[3] According to Bartels we may distinguish six different periods in the history of marketing thought since its 'discovery' between 1900 and 1910. In Bartels's view, prior to 1900 market behaviour and trade practice were explained mainly from the macro viewpoint in economic theory. However, while the emphasis upon scientific management, exemplified *inter alia* by the studies of Frederick Taylor, diverted attention from the public to private economic problems virtually no attention was given to the distribution activity. As a result, as Bartels points out, there developed

> a gap in theoretical explanation as social and economic conditions departed increasingly from the assumptions concerning the market on which existing trade theory was built. Competition no longer characterised some markets: demanders and suppliers were farther removed from each other; customary relations of demand and supply were becoming reversed; and new patterns of living were evolving. New interpretations of economic activity were needed, as were new applications of management science to distributive business. These needs nurtured the discovery of marketing.

Thus Bartels's period of *discovery* may be summarised as a period in which the early teachers of the subject sought facts about the distributive trades. In the process of this search, theory was borrowed mainly from economics, particularly in the fields of distribution, world trade and commodity markets, and the term 'marketing' was selected to describe this particular activity.

The years between 1910 and 1920 are characterised by Bartels as a period of *conceptualisation,* and in this era 'basic concepts on which the structure of marketing thought was built for the next forty or fifty years emerged and were crystallised'. It was during this period that many marketing concepts were initially developed and classified and terms defined. It was also during this time that three lines of approach to the analysis of marketing were identified – the institutional, the functional and the commodity approaches. Significant amongst early contributions to the functional approach are the writings of Shaw, Weld and Cherington.[4]

Weld also contributed to the institutional approach as did Paul H. Nystrom whose *Retail Selling and Store Management* and *The Economics of Retailing* did much to elucidate the operation and structural elements associated with retail distribution.[5] Many other notable contributions were made during this period relating to advertising, the provision of credit, selling and sales management, and so on, and the reader seeking a description of these is recommended to refer to Bartels for a detailed review.

Following on the many and diverse contributions made during the decade from 1910 to 1920 the next decade is characterised as a *period of integration*. As Bartels comments, 'the years between 1920 and 1930 mark the coming of age of the discipline of marketing. During that decade not only did all the branches of the subject attain a general or integrated statement, but two additional areas of specialisation appeared – wholesaling and marketing research.' At this stage of its development the marketing concept was defined as comprising 'all of those activities involved in the distribution of goods from producers to consumers and in the transfer of title thereto'. It is not surprising therefore that the emphasis was again placed upon the physical activities such as wholesaling, retailing and their relationship to one another in the concept of a marketing channel. However, during the 1930s changes in social and economic conditions had a marked effect moulding the direction of thinking and practice in marketing with the result that Bartels describes the 1930s and 1940s as a *period of development*. Synoptically this phase is characterised as one during which 'specialised areas of marketing continued to be developed, hypothetical assumptions were verified and quantified, and some new approaches to the explanation of marketing were undertaken'. In turn, the developments of the 1930s laid the basis for the next decade – typified as a *period of reappraisal*. It was probably during this period that academics and other thinkers concerned with the development of marketing began to ask themselves whether the body of knowledge had achieved, or could aspire to, the status of a science. With the benefit of hindsight it would seem fair to say that by 1950 marketing thinking encompassed an impressive array of content and techniques that was short of concepts and certainly lacked any general theory or theories of marketing. It was with these latter issues that we have been concerned in the second half of the twentieth century commencing with Bartels's *period of conceptualisation* (1950–60) which he summarises as being the period during which 'traditional approaches to the study of marketing were supplemented by increasing emphasis upon managerial decision making, the societal aspects of marketing, and quantitative marketing analysis. Many new concepts, some borrowed from the field of management, some from the other social sciences, were introduced into marketing.'

In Halbert's opinion the evolution of marketing thought described by Bartels has been accompanied by a shift in both approach and method *vis-à-vis* marketing theory. Thus there has been a shift from:

1. Subjective approaches to objective ones.
2. Less formalised approaches to more theoretical ones (models, mathematics, statistics, marketing research).
3. The qualitative to the quantitative, even in unlikely areas of attitudes, opinions, and motivations (scaling, and projective techniques).
4. Rigorous classifications to gradations and refinements.
5. Classification to causation.
6. Static to dynamic theories (classical statistical approaches, to Markov processes simulation).
7. Disjointed facts and descriptions to a search for generalisations, principles, theories, and laws.
8. Surface analysis to depth investigations.
9. Sheer speculation (which is necessary) to realism and more directly applicable concepts and theories.[6]

Throughout this process the budding marketing theorist has drawn heavily upon other disciplines, especially economics, the behavioural sciences and, more recently, the management sciences. We conclude this chapter by considering the relationship between marketing and these source disciplines in slightly greater depth as a basis for the detailed review of the selected marketing areas discussed in Part 2.

Marketing and Economics

As indicated earlier, the study of marketing developed as a branch of applied economics concerned with the study of channels of distribution. Thus the macroeconomic model of resource allocation recognises four principal activities:

(1) Extractive and agrarian;
(2) Manufacturing, assembling and fabricating;
(3) Distribution; and
(4) Consumption.

The model locates marketing in the third category. Within such a scheme, marketing is viewed as part of the theory of economic allocation and its contribution is considered to be the creation of value through time, place and possession utilities.

However, while the study of distribution in economics was concerned with flows at the macro level, marketing is concerned primarily with micro flows of goods and services between organisations and persons. Accordingly, borrowing from economics has tended to be concentrated more upon price and output theory and has drawn heavily upon such concepts as 'price elasticity', 'market equilibrium', 'diminishing marginal utility', 'economies of scale', and so on.

Marketing has also made frequent use of the concept of 'economic man' which holds that purchasing decisions are largely the result of rational and economic calculations on the part of the buyer. However, as Halbert comments, 'Economic man is assumed to have full and complete information about the decision under consideration. In classical economics when the problem of price is being considered, it is assumed that all customers and all suppliers know the location of all products, and that the information about price, quality, quantity, and availability is instantly available and completely correct.'[7] Such simplifying assumptions are essential to the development of a theory which has proved of enormous value, as both a general statement of how the price mechanism operates under changing conditions of supply and demand, as well as specifying which variables need to be monitored in the real world if the model is to have practical application.

However, the economist's emphasis upon a single equilibrium

point ignores several facets of behaviour which are of central importance to the marketer. The economist has not concerned himself with the manner in which preferences are formed, nor how they are rank-ordered, both of which constitute a major preoccupation of marketing practitioners. Similarly, economists are not concerned with the manner in which preferences may be psychologically modified or altered by new stimuli, yet this area is a major preoccupation of advertising and sales-promotional efforts. In the same manner, economics pays scant attention to the interaction between buyer and seller in the negotiation of a sale – yet another vital area for the marketing man.

In essence, therefore, economics provides a rich source of theory, concepts and ideas but is an inadequate explanation of the real world. Indeed, if it were an adequate explanation of the real world it is very doubtful that there would have been a need for the new composite discipline of marketing. Fundamentally the inadequacy of economic theory rests on the concept of 'rationality', the definition of which is tautologous, as is apparent in this quotation from Halbert:

> The concept of rationality, so central to economic theory on examination, appears to be a very difficult concept indeed. If we define rationality as behaviour designed to maximise utility and then define utility as that which behaviour tends to maximise, we are not very far ahead.

Clearly, the marketer is in need of a better explanation of behaviour than this and it is for this reason that he has also borrowed extensively from the behavioural sciences.

Marketing and the Behavioural Sciences

In Halbert's view the major contribution of the behavioural sciences – amongst which may be numbered anthropology, demography, political science, psychology and sociology – lies not so much in specific techniques or ideas but in the fact that they require 'that marketing science take explicit account of the human and social aspects of individuals and groups engaged in marketing behaviour'.[8]

While this is not to say that marketing cannot borrow specific concepts, such as stimulus–response models or Freudian psychodynamic personality theory, it underlines the fact that the behavioural sciences have tried to grapple with the complexity and uncertainty implicit in the real world rather than assume much of it away as the economists have done. Thus it is from the behavioural scientist's *approach* that marketing theorists and researchers probably have most to learn. At the same time it should also be recognised that marketing has made many notable contributions of its own in the methodology of social surveys since it first adopted these techniques, and it is not overstating the situation to claim that nowadays marketing researchers are leaders in the development of new techniques. However, the warning sounded in the previous chapter must also be recognised – namely that preoccupation with techniques, especially in a pseudo-experimental setting of the marketing laboratory, may tempt us to ignore the real world outside.

Another major contribution of the behavioural sciences is its treatment of values and their effect upon human behaviour, especially in the context of decision-taking. Thus, while decision theory provides a logically compelling framework for analysis, its utility is constrained to the extent that we can identify and measure values. In this context the behavioural sciences have made a signal contribution by pointing out that while people tend to obey the pleasure/pain principle by maximising the former and avoiding the latter, none the less people tend to like what they do – not only do what they like. In other words, a person's values may be as much conditioned by his behaviour as the other way around. Certainly, values change over time and marketing has made its own contribution to the sociologists' and anthropologists' studies of maturation and changing value systems with its concept of 'life-style' and consumption behaviour.

In fact, marketing has drawn extensively upon the behavioural sciences in developing its own specialism of consumer behaviour, which is the subject of Chapter 4, as well as the field of marketing communications (Chapter 5) and diffusion of innovations (Chapter 7). Accordingly, further discussion is deferred at this juncture.

Marketing and the Management Sciences

A study of the development of 'management science' is felt to have particular relevance to the marketing theorist and, at the very least, he should read chapter 9 of Halbert's book. This view is predicated by the observation that in many ways management scientists have achieved that which marketing scientists are seeking – acceptance and recognition in their own right – within the past twenty to thirty years. Further, they appear to have done this by the same processes of borrowing, synthetising and integration which reflect the efforts of marketing scientists. Thus Halbert notes that

> Their [management scientists and operation researchers] activities have been characterised by emphasis on the mathematical modeling of systems and the development of decision rules for making 'optimal' choices among alternative courses of action. Their techniques have been drawn from a wide variety of disciplines, including applied mathematics, economics, statistics, and psychology.[9]

One might comment that of these disciplines psychology is probably least in evidence and that the early acceptance of management science owes much to its concentration on 'soluble' problems in which the key variables could be both specified and quantified. More recently, management science has turned to less tractable problems incorporating judgement and uncertainty, and thus more characteristic of marketing situations. In these areas their success and credibility is of a much lower order. This is not to argue that the techniques and methods of the econometrician, operation researcher and management scientist are without value – it merely underlines the normal human propensity to solve the easy problems first and defer consideration of the more difficult issues.

It is our view that the emergence of a discipline of marketing represents a conscious attempt to grapple with and explain the real world and that we should not be discouraged if progress is both painful and slow. That progress has been made is readily apparent in the contributions to Part 2 of this book and we should take heart from this rather than be overly impressed with the initial acceptance accorded management science and so attempt to emulate it. Certainly, this danger is apparent in the emphasis upon experimentation outlined in Chapter 2 which has contributed little to a real understanding of the problem of how advertising works.

To conclude this part of the book, therefore, we would defend marketing's borrowing from other disciplines on the grounds that the emergence of a study of marketing stems largely from a failure of these disciplines to borrow from each other and to integrate economic and behavioural concepts into an acceptable explanation of the real world. Marketing may not have achieved this – and may never achieve it – but it is clearly a goal worth pursuing.

Part 2
Evolution of Marketing Thought

Chapter 4

Towards a Theory of Consumer Behaviour

INTRODUCTION

Consumer behaviour is a comparatively new field of study. In this chapter is presented a historical perspective of the development of interest in this area, followed by a consideration of the current search for a general framework for analysis of consumer actions, based upon concepts and models borrowed from a variety of source disciplines. An exposition of the major comprehensive models which have now been constructed completes the outline of the theoretical basis.

Having isolated the relevent influential variables in the purchase decision, the implications for the marketing practitioner are considered. By empirical testing, the manner in which these variables affect the ultimate outcome of a consumer decision process is shown to clarify and to enrich theory and practice together.

HISTORICAL PERSPECTIVES

Markcting as a management function has emerged from a realisation by business that the consumer is the *sine qua non* of every activity of the business – that consumer orientation which forms the substance of the marketing concept has as its objective the direction of the efforts of the enterprise towards the service of customers at a profit.

The need for a marketing function, separate and defined, was a consequence of the changing structure of the production sector of the economy from small localised industries to the large-scale production plants. An intimate and personal knowledge of the customer had characterised the craftsman era, en-

An ultimate a personal knowledge of the customer had characterized the craftsman era

abling products to be tailored to meet the known requirements of the individual consumer. Mass-production techniques demanded product consistency so that the craftsman's instinctive appreciation of his customers' unique representation of what constituted satisfaction was an apparent anachronism, and as such was neglected during the early stages of modern industrial society. So long as a sellers' market prevailed in the consumer-goods field, the intricacies and complexities associated with producing to meet consumer desires could indeed be ignored with equanimity. Any reversal of economic conditions, however, which would allow for the buyer to exercise personal preferences by making choices between fiercely competing brands and products, would inevitably re-establish as a meaningful competitive tool a business philosophy aimed at producing goods to meet customers' requirements.

Just such a *volte-face* did in fact come about in most western economies after the end of the Second World War. During the war fundamental and permanent changes had been brought about in the economic structure. Income patterns had been re-shaped, with a consequent expansion in that section of the consuming public with a level of income in excess of their immediate needs. Greater discretionary income was not the only distinguishing trait of the post-war consumer. Modes and availability of credit raised access to funds above the level of current income; at the same time, mass-media channels were disseminating product information on a large scale. The modern consumer then was both wealthier and more knowledgeable than his pre-war counterpart. The element of discretion he was able to introduce into his consumption patterns changed his role from a passive spectator to an active participant in the economic scene.

Change had not been restricted to the consumer. On the production side, the effect of the large-scale units had been steadily to widen the gap between the individual producer and the individual consumer. Markets for the manufacturer's output were no longer local and personal; communications had become impersonal and competitive activity flourished. Such an economic situation provided the impetus for the revival of business interest in the actions of the consumer.

Katona,[1] working on consumer surveys at the University of Michigan, put forward the suggestion that consumer purchase decisions could be better understood if concepts of psychology and economics were combined. The basic principle of his psychological economics theory was the dimension of 'willingness to buy' as a determinant of purchase action: 'Discretionary demand is a function of both ability to buy and willingness to buy.' His explanation of this basic concept stated that 'Income, previously accumulated financial assets and access to credit constitute ability to buy, and thereby the conditions without which inclinations to buy cannot be transformed into demand. Willingness to buy is represented by psychological predispositions in the individual who makes the purchase.'[2]

A decade or so later Andrew Shonfield similarly emphasised the inadequacy inherent in applying an unqualified economic approach to business activity. Writing in *The Times*, he commented that 'it is arguable that the disappointment with our current performance in the management of the economy is the result of expecting economics to do on its own a job that requires a joint and massive effort by the whole range of social sciences'.[3]

From the consumer surveys undertaken by the University of Michigan has emanated a more dynamic perspective of the individual purchase decision, with the influences of past experience and future expectations being clearly demonstrated. Further, these surveys have amply disclosed evidence of the gradual processes of social learning, as well as the impact of changing social attitudes upon consumption patterns. Credit usage, as a case in point, has detached itself completely from the old stigma attached to hire purchase, with the use of many forms of credit now being an overt and socially acceptable method of planning one's own consumption timing.

The past decade has seen a complementary, but more direct, cause for taking an interest in the consumer, arising from the rapid growth of the consumer movement. Consumers have themselves become aware of the power they wield in a highly competitive economic situation. Resulting from this public awareness of the importance of the consumer in the business game, governments in all western countries have openly declared that the system does not always operate to the benefit of the individual consumer, and statutory consumer-protection agencies have been created. Legislation at this stage is almost entirely protective in nature, aimed at redressing what is seen as the imbalance between the large-scale, impersonal production units and the individual consumer. Looking to the future, however, governments recognise the desirability of consumer-education programmes. The value attached to reliable information in assisting the consumer to reach a satisfactory purchase decision has already come under close scrutiny, with standards being set for the advertising industry as a whole.

GENERAL FRAMEWORK FOR THE ANALYSIS OF CONSUMER ACTIONS

This combined drive of a legislative climate which is sympathetic towards the consumer interest, and the growing cognisance of the central significance of the customer to the activities of the business, has turned the attention of practitioners and theoreticians alike to the search for a general framework which can aid the understanding of the observed actions of individuals in the consumption role. Systematic research in this field is in its early days, and is founded upon an eclectic approach to the established behavioural disciplines.

To develop an initial framework from which a unified theory of consumer behaviour can grow, concepts have in the first instance been borrowed from those fields of study concerned with the totality of human behaviour – economics, psychology, sociology and anthropology in the main. The purpose of such borrowing is to relate these concepts to the purchase decision-making process of the individual consumer, so that as the theory progresses, the varied strands of thought can become integrated into a single, cogent multidisciplinary area. Consumer-behaviour theory accentuates the purchase decision-making process, with the underlying rationale that those variables which can be identified as being salient to the decision process can be applied to the design of more effective marketing programmes. The introductory fragmented borrowing of existing concepts from other areas has now been superseded as the main line of advancement in consumer research by the attempts by marketers to construct general and experimental models depicting the interrelationships between those variables which impinge upon the individual consumer before, during, and even after, the act of purchase. The influences concerned are those which have been drawn from other behavioural sources. What is new is the conceptualisation of the manner in which these pre-identified factors affect the outcome of the purchase decision process by the manipulation of the informational input.

Models generally provide a useful framework and guide to further research by the clarification of relevant relationships. Consumer-behaviour models particularise the relationships existing between inputs into the buying situation, the social and individual motivations which are present in the situation, and the resultant outcome. This outcome may be positive or negative – a decision to make a purchase or a decision to reject a product. There are, therefore, obvious advantages to the construction of models at this point in the evolution of a theory of consumer behaviour. The measure of logic in the construct highlights the total picture of a decision process, as well as indicating the contribution of each portion of the model to the whole picture. A frame of reference is created against which consumer problems can be set, with all the major variables both classified and clearly stated. Against that, however, are the disadvantages associated with modelling techniques related to human behaviour. One danger is that complex situations may be oversimplified in terms of the model, with the less intricate representation of the model being substituted in marketing planning for the more complicated reality.

Modelling of the purchase decision process followed from the isolated extreme perspectives of psychology and economics. Psychology concentrated upon the uniqueness of the individual response to inputs, whilst economics emphasised relative homogeneity by working in aggregates. Psychological thought provided the basis for the original 'black-box' model, which portrays an individual actively involved in the manipulation of a system of inputs and outputs. Stimuli (informational inputs) enter into the black box, where they are in some abstruse way processed via the individual's psychological character – composed of such factors as personality, cognitions, motivations and attitudes. As a consequence, some kind of behavioural output occurs. The precise happenings within this individual and unique black box have given rise to speculation and experimentation for many years.

Economics, on the other hand, has produced a theory of utility, or satisfaction, where the purchase decision process is viewed as the consumer's efforts to maximise his over-all level of

47

by the manner in which he distributes his income
of goods and services. The buying behaviour of the
nomic man is not influenced by such factors as con-
time or lack of appropriate information; nor is any
a... made for his desire to attain social or emotional
satisfaction from his purchases.

COMPREHENSIVE MODELS OF CONSUMER BEHAVIOUR

Contemporary consumer models owe much of their basic
structure to contributions drawn from models of human behaviour previously hypothesised by a variety of branches of the
social sciences. Traces of these pioneering thoughts are readily
discernible in the major experimental consumer models present-
ly extant.

Allport's[4] investigations into prejudice illuminated areas of
influence, both from within the individual and also occasioned
by his contacts with his social environment, which can be shown
to affect the perception of an object stimulus. Prejudice was
defined by Allport as 'a feeling, favorable or unfavorable,
toward a person or thing, prior to, or not based on actual
experience', which equates closely with current opinions on the
effect of subjective predispositions upon the outcome of an individual's purchase decision process.

The well-known psychoanalytic perspective of human behaviour is attributable to the efforts of Freud[5] in revealing the
different levels of consciousness which make up the individual
psyche. Emphasis here was placed upon the impact of the
deeper levels of consciousness upon the decision process,
motivated by a need structure which the individual is striving
to satisfy. Motivation can be understood as the driving-force
input into the decision process, with output being described as
the attainment of the specific goal towards which the individual
is propelled by an unsatisfied need operating at a subconscious
level.

Veblen's[6] model concentrates upon the interaction of the
individual with his social environment by stressing that all
human behaviour takes place within the wider social context.
Individual behaviour can best be understood as being aimed at

a desire for social satisfaction. Veblen's viewpoint has stimulated research into the pressures upon the individual to conform to the norms of the family and friends composing his social world. Social conformity has been shown to be of value as an explanatory element of some of the manipulative processes which informational input undergoes as the individual moves towards a decision outcome.

The suggestion that human behaviour is learned behaviour was propounded by Pavlov[7] as the basis for a theory of classical conditioning. Experimenting with dogs, he established that any two things presented together will be permanently associated together in the cognitive system. With the constant reinforcement of consecutive presentation of the associated objects, a given stimulus will elicit the expected behavioural response.

A final pioneering area in extending knowledge of human behaviour stems from the work undertaken by psychologists of the *Gestalt* school. *Gestalt* psychology recognises that a major function of the cognitive system is to relate perceptual stimuli to each other and to the environment in order to create an organised and comprehensible world. This is the setting used by Lewin[8] in advancing an explanatory model of human behaviour. The individual decision process operates within a total situation which includes an individual need structure and interaction between the individual and the external environment. Needs can be satisfied through a range of actions, and behaviour results from the evaluation of the positive and negative aspects (as perceived by the individual) related to each possible course of action. A wider discussion of the contribution of behaviour models to the understanding of consumer actions has been developed by Kotler,[9] from whom the above analysis is largely derived.

The fabrication of the more comprehensive models of consumer behaviour has been stimulated by the combination of these observed behavioural factors with the long-standing microeconomic constructs originating with the classical utility theory proposed by Marshall.[10]

Figure 4.1 summarises the present stage of thinking in the consumer-behaviour field. This is intended as a simplified graphical representation of those factors which have been identified as exerting pressure at some point in the decision process. Relative strengths and the interrelationships which undoubtedly exist between the variables are not within the compass of this diagram, which has as its purpose the delineation of those factors which have been shown to be influential.

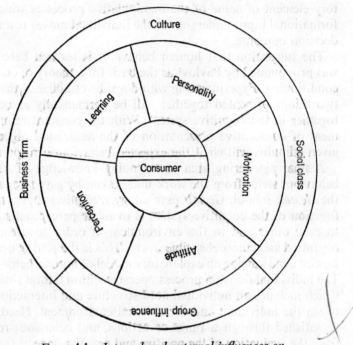

FIG. 4.1 *Internal and external influences on the consumer decision process*

In the first instance, these factors can be dichotomised into internal and external influences upon the individual which affect the outcome of a purchase decision. Internal factors refer to those arising from within the individual's unique psychological make-up. Personality and attitude, motivation, perception and the total cognitive system can be expected to be brought into play to produce a purchase action.

External factors, which are sometimes referred to as the environmental forces to which the individual is perpetually subjected, exist in terms of aggregates rather than in the individual sense. It is obvious that consumption patterns are affected by culture, or by social-class belonging, by group affiliations and the impact of personal influence. These influences have been shown to be capable of producing extreme distortion of business communications both in the receptivity of the individual and in his method of processing the inputs.

The comprehensive models now to be presented all have as a basis these same fundamental variable groups. Structuring a purchase decision process involves the individual and his environment, with a third essential element being the business firm which initiates the process by some form of marketing communication. Amongst the better-known of the comprehensive models which serve to illustrate the manner in which consumer behaviour theory is advancing are those constructed by Nicosia,[11] Andreasen,[12] Engel, Kollat and Blackwell,[13] Clawson,[14] and Howard and Sheth.[15] These models differ in respect to their complexity and orientation but are nevertheless based upon the same strands of thought. Thus similarities are to be found in the isolation and identification of the relevant variables, and in the perspective of a dynamic decision process, with the actions of the consumer viewed as a movement towards some decision point.

Nicosia

Nicosia uses as a base for his model a computer flow chart technique, divided into four distinct areas, or 'fields'. The output from each field becomes the input to the succeeding field.

The model depicts a message (for example an advertisement for a new product) flowing from its source (in this case, the business firm) in the direction of an eventual decision outcome by the consumer. In Field One the consumer is exposed to and receives the message, with an outcome of the development of some predisposition, or attitude, towards the product. Field Two is concerned with the search and evaluation process, which has as its output the arousal of the individual's motivation, leading to Field Three which is defined as 'possible transformation of the motivation into an act of purchase'. If purchase occurs, Field Four becomes the area of storage and use of the product, with a related output of experience.

In each of the fields, the relevant influences upon the eventual outcome are delineated. As the message flows from the business firm to the formation of a consumer attitude, it will be modified or distorted by internal subjective perceptual elements. During the period of 'search and evaluation' (Field Two) the internal and external forces are differentiated in terms of additional information input. Internally initiated data are concerned with the associations, conscious or unconscious, with the firm, the brand or the product, whilst external data are culled from the environment in the form of word-of-mouth communication, or an increased receptivity to advertising in the product area.

Andreasen

Andreasen has developed the concepts of 'attitude formation' and 'attitude change', contributed by social psychologists, to construct a consumer decision model as an information-processing cycle. This model indicates that attitude change can be achieved via exposure to information. Change of attitude is assumed to be a logical preliminary to a change in behaviour, an assumption which is lacking in verification since the complexity of the attitude–behaviour relationship remains a controversial area in social-psychology studies. It is as yet far from certain that influence in this area is a one-way flow from attitude to behaviour as the model suggests.

Andreasen's model centres upon the individual utilising a message input to reach a decision outcome, with attitude formation and change as the central concepts. The predispositional nature of attitudes (that is, 'not based on actual experience')[16] is shown to impinge upon the individual's perceptions, which operate as a filter through which the information must pass to reach the cognitive system. Thus attitudes to message source or channel may effectively alter the character of the original communication.

Engel, Kollat and Blackwell

Described as a complete model of buying behaviour, these researchers have produced a sequential approach to the purchase decision. It is a general model which gives a framework for examining the diverse range of influences to which the buyer is subject as the decision process moves from its initial stage of the beginnings of need awareness through its subsequent steps up to the terminal stage of after-the-event evaluation and rationalisation. The contributions of the three basic internal processes – perception, learning and motivation – represent major steps in the model, whilst personality and attitudes are seen to exert pressure upon the process. The social and cultural aspects of the possible purchase decision are also shown as influencing the individual's movement through the decision stages.

Clawson

Clawson has extended the views propounded by Lewin in his behavioural studies, with the contribution of *Gestalt* theories clearly in evidence.

The analysis is concentrated in some depth upon the tension element in a purchase decision as the individual assesses the positive and the negative aspects attached to the decision outcome, producing a situation of psychic conflict. The fact that both the positive and the negative features are perceived subjectively by the consumer is also stressed, indicating that the conflict cannot be resolved on the grounds of objective product characteristics or information. These objective criteria may not penetrate the net of selective perception, or may be distorted on the way.

Howard and Sheth

Howard and Sheth have based their approach to the formulation of a general consumer model on the standpoint of the consumer playing an active role in the business transaction. He is not merely exposed to communications but is portrayed as vigorously collecting and processing information.

Fundamentally, the model is constructed around a series of stimulus variables passing into the individual's processing system and being acted upon by the internal factors of perception and learning, termed by the researchers 'the hypothetical constructs'. A response variable terminates the process, with the whole being surrounded by the exogenous variables of social class, culture and personality, plus such constraints as time and income availability.

Inputs are separated out into three groups which distinguish source differences. The first group of inputs relates to the actual product communications of price, quality, availability, distinctiveness and service. The second group derives from indirect and impersonal sources, such as salesmen or the mass media. The third group of stimulus variables identifies the activity of the consumer collecting data from his social environment via the personal influence of word-of-mouth communication. Thus the interaction between the consumer and his social environment is distinguished and extended, showing the external forces in the decision process not only as a constraint upon behaviour, but also as a reference point for the gathering of credible information. Interaction between man and his social environment is seen to be a two-way function.

The hypothetical constructs of perception and learning detail the manipulation of the information gathered from the various sources, affecting the amount and quality of objective information which reaches the system.

Howard and Sheth have acknowledged that these hypothetical constructs and their interrelationships are a consequence of the integration of a number of well-known theories – Hull's learning theory, Osgood's cognitive theory and Berlyne's theory of exploratory behaviour.

Although as can be seen from this brief review of the major experimental models, the theory of consumer behaviour has shown significant advances; no model of buying behaviour can be considered as an end in itself. 'Markets are dynamic phenomena, and changes in market response should be expected.'[17] Therefore, to be of value in the planning of marketing strategies, models can provide a basis for methodical thinking, but must retain sufficient flexibility to constantly adapt to the changing environment. The purpose of the model is to reflect reality, not to replace it.

MARKETING APPLICATIONS OF CONSUMER-BEHAVIOUR THEORY

Consumer behaviour at present can offer but an immature general theory, the practical applications of which may not be immediately evident. Pragmatism being the essence of marketing, the consequent emphasis upon expediency by the marketing practitioner presents an opportune situation for the 'theory–

the perceived price differences and consistently underestimated the strength with which consumers view the importance of service and warranty, ease of use and style. It is of some import that such perceptual differences were revealed even within this relatively personalised retailer–customer relationship.

Consumer versus marketer perceptions of a new package design was the focus of Blum and Appel's study,[22] with a wide discrepancy apparent between the two perspectives on the basis of consumer and management reaction to eighteen different package designs. It was concluded that if the package decision had been made by management, 'the net effect would have been to select designs which would have had the least appeal so far as the consumers sampled were concerned'.

That non-objective phenomena can be expected to influence consumer perception of physical product attributes is axiomatic in the light of the universal consensus of the subjective nature of perception. A proliferation of studies has been conducted around this concept of perceived product characteristics, including a number of taste tests designed to disclose the effect of a well-known brand name upon perceived quality. Makens[23] found that when identical samples of turkey meat were labelled with a well-known and an unknown brand, the sample with the known brand label was perceived as being of higher quality. Continuing the experiment with two unmarked samples, this time of differing quality, the superior meat was 'recognised' as the well-known brand. A similar type of experiment by Brown[24] used identically fresh loaves of bread, some wrapped in cellophane and some in wax paper. Those loaves wrapped in cellophane were judged to be the fresher.

That social values influence perception was exposed by Haire's[25] well-known enquiry into the meaning attached by housewives to instant and regular coffee. Users of instant coffee were perceived as 'lazy', and as failing to measure up to a socially determined and socially accepted good-housewife standard.

Social psychologists have observed, as previously noted, that it is not possible for the human being to perceive and internalise the multiplicity of sensory stimulation with which he is surrounded. Bauer and Greyser[26] applied this concept to the field of advertising. Out of a potential exposure of some 1500 advertisements per day, the consumer was found in this study to actually perceive only 76, and perhaps 12 of these could be related to his subsequent behaviour.

Learning

Interest in learning theories stems from Pavlov's early work in classical conditioning which broadly established that much human behaviour is learned behaviour. Learning in this context can be defined formally as 'all changes in behaviour that result from previous behaviour in similar situations'.[27] Learning theory becomes applicable in the context of consumer action, where in numerous purchasing situations the behavioural outcome can be related to past experience.

Although there has been some dispute in the source discipline regarding the simple form of learning theory – a temporal contiguity of stimulus and response leading to the formation of an associative bond – the application of the concept of behavioural learning resulting from past experience to the repetitive buying situation, and to the development of brand loyalty, has generated an interesting segment of empirical research effort.

Reinforcement of stimulus was a central feature of the classical conditioning model, and it is this area of message repetition which has been the most assiduously examined, giving rise to the general observation that distribution of an advertisement over a period of time is more effective in achieving perception and retention than a heavy concentration of the same advertisement in a limited time period.

This generalisation has, however, been subject to modification. Myers and Reynolds[28] conclude from their research studies that continuity of an advertising campaign over a period of time is more effective for an established product, whilst for a new product, which requires some thought on the part of the consumer, a greater impact can be achieved through concentrating the message repetition into a short time span, which is in accord with the views of psychologists regarding established patterns of behaviour (that is previously learned behaviour), and the formation of new patterns of behaviour.

Krugman[29] studied the effects of repeated exposure to packaging in order to establish the frequency with which an object must be seen to become familiar. He drew attention to the tendency for consumer research to be 'based on responses to single rather than repeated exposure to products, packaging and advertising copy – despite an enormous body of evidence indicating that such responses change with experience and the passage of time'.

A major consideration to emerge from the study of message repetition is the determination of the critical point at which any further repetition appears to lead to a negative response, or negative learning taking place. That this critical point exists has been indicated by Cox[30] and Bogart.[31] Attempts to determine and generalise the exact location of this critical point have proved inconclusive. Whilst for one product repetition of the message up to eight times continued to have an accelerating effect, at the other extreme the point of decay occurred after only four exposures for a different product.[32] Clearly, exposure to the advertisement is not the sole factor affecting the level of interest of the consumer. Variations in creative presentation have been suggested as a major element; the particular product groups concerned may also be a determinant of the critical point.

A long-standing proposition in this sphere of retention and learning is that 'the greater the complexity and length of the message the greater will be the amount of repetition necessary for it to be perceived and retained'.[33] Confirmation of this proposition has been provided, notably by communications psychologists Hovland, Janis and Kelley,[34] and by advertising researcher Bogart.[35]

Competition and its effect upon the required measure of message reinforcement extend the application of learning theory into the reality of the business world. Underwood's[36] findings in this connection have indicated that interference from competing messages may be the major factor in the advertisement being forgotten.

The practical value of ascertaining the most effective repetition level and time period for a specific promotional campaign needs no elaboration.

Probabilistic models have evolved to provide a wider description of the learning process, using two fundamental assumptions:

(1) Present behaviour is influenced by past behaviour; and

(2) Recent events are more influential than less recent events.

Kuehn[37] used a stochastic learning model technique to predict purchases of orange juice. The conclusions from this study indicate that brand loyalty is at its strongest amongst the most frequent purchasers of orange juice, and that brand preference weakens as time between purchases increases. Furthermore, for this particular product it was found that brand loyalties are never so strong that complete acceptance or rejection of any one brand can be assumed automatically.

Personality

Empirical studies verifying the impact of personality upon the consumer decision process have been much less decisive, and to date the use of personality as a predictive variable in consumer actions has proved to be most unsatisfactory. The evidence available is a confusion of mainly negative and contradictory findings. One reason for such discouraging results may well be the surfeit of measuring instruments, which all purport to measure this same variable of personality. As a consequence, research in this area has been atomistic and non-comparable.

A comment by Hall and Lindzey[38] confirms this lack of uniformity in defining personality: 'no substantive definition of personality can be applied with any generality . . . personality is defined by the particular empirical concepts which are a part of the theory of personality applied by the observer'. Turning to the source area, it is noticeable that, in their classic review of behavioural theory and research, Berelson and Steiner[39] do not include a separate section on personality.

However, Tucker[40] has stated that it would be premature at this stage for marketers to minimise the role of personality in the consumer decision process. He suggests rather that this variable warrants more vigorous attention, perhaps including the development of personality measures which are more closely related to purchase behaviour. Brody and Cunningham[41] are in agreement with this suggestion. As a result of their studies in this area, they argue that the current lack of any revealed relationship between personality and consumer actions is not an indicator that no such relationships exist. Rather it pinpoints the lack of any adequate framework within which to analyse this relationship.

Motivation

Motivation, as conceptualised by Nicosia,[42] acts as a driving force in the flow towards purchase action; but as an empirical research variable it has been found difficult to render operational. Lindzey[43] outlines the problem in his comment that 'the conceptual nature of motivational variables has remained so murky that even the clear distinction of these variables from other classes of concepts employed in psychological theory is yet to be accomplished'.

Research into the role of motivation has attempted to discover the underlying and subconscious reasons for purchase actions, analysed within a framework of Freudian theory. Businessmen particularly have expressed doubt about the practical applicability of the conclusions from these studies.

The main proponents of motivation research have been Dichter[44] and Henry;[45] the major contribution from their work has been the expansion of the tools of traditional market research to include the use of indirect and unstructured techniques.

As yet, then, motivation is viewed as a non-operational variable, but interest in this area could well be revived by the development of Lewin's theories into the general model constructed by Clawson. The individual need structure is a central feature of this field of study.

Attitude

Attitude is a concept which has been contributed to the theory of consumer behaviour by social psychology. It is commonly considered to represent a predisposition on the part of the individual to take action. Since attitude research has commanded a significant investment of resources, there is clearly an expectation that attitudes will in fact be found to be reliable predictors of consumer action.

Whether such faith is warranted is a matter of dissent between researchers in the area. Conclusive substantiation of the causal link between attitude and subsequent behaviour has not yet been achieved. An energetic researcher into this area of attitudes is Fishbein.[46] Basing his views upon an exhaustive study of the seventy-five years of attitudinal research, he questions the validity of the underlying assumption of this research area, namely that attitudes towards a product or an object have a direct link with behaviour. Similar misgivings are affirmed by Bird and Ehrenberg:[47]

> the interplay between attitude change and behavioural change is as yet very unclear despite the large and increasing amounts of money and effort put into the assessment of consumer attitudes and motives. There is in fact little data available on the relation between change in attitude and changes in behaviour.

A study by Barclay[48] used a semantic differential scale to examine how well brand attitudes compared with a measure of purchasing behaviour. The product category was a typical mass-consumption food item with the general characteristics of high purchase frequency relatively low unit price, and a large number of apparently homogeneous competing brands. The measured attitudes to brands were not found to relate to actual purchasing behaviour (that is brands purchased in the past month). Barclay comments that

> it should not be expected that brand attitudes alone would be strongly associated with purchasing behaviour. Such market place variables as temporary out-of-stock of the favored brand, price dealing of competitive brands, etc., surely exert a critical influence on actual purchasing.

Udell[49] on the other hand restates Allport's original view that attitudes exert a strong influence upon behaviour, observing that 'attitude research offers a potentially useful device for explaining and predicting consumer behaviour. Furthermore, a knowledge of consumer attitudes may provide a sound basis for improving products, redesigning packages, and developing and evaluating promotional programs'. Udell's study was designed to determine the public's attitude toward trading stamps, using four selected cities. More important, though, 'the research sought to determine what relationship existed between consumer's attitudes and their behaviour concerning trading stamps'. The research tool was the Thurstone technique, designed to provide both a qualitative and a quantitative measurement. Support for the theory of an attitude-behaviour link comes also from Andreasen, whose comprehensive consumer model has attitude formation and change as a central concept.

Culture

As an influential factor in the decision process, and in the formation of consumption patterns, the study of culture has presented peculiar difficulties. Anthropologists have agreed that culture is not easy to define in specific discernible and measureable components since the term represents an over-all social heritage, a distinctive form of environmental adaptation by a whole society of people. The pervasive nature of cultural influence is a force shaping both patterns of consumption and patterns of decision-making from infancy; it both describes and prescribes the way of life of the specific society. Actions and thoughts are shaped and limited by the pertinent culture which, by permitting certain actions, thoughts and feelings, makes increasingly unlikely contradictory or tangential behaviour.

Due to this relative indefinability in operational terms, research efforts aimed at isolating the existence of a cultural impact upon consumer actions has focused upon examinations of the clear-cut variations between consumption habits in different societies and countries.

In addition, the effects of culture upon perception have been revealed. White[50] has related this concept of culturally bound perception to advertising, stressing the initial need for advertising to understand, reflect and accept the value structure of society before setting about its creative task of organising the numerous stimulations a product contains for a particular customer. Advertising, concludes White, 'can operate within the limits of culture to create new expectations for the consumer'.

Social Class

Sociology has established that relationships exist between social class and consumption patterns. Witness this summary by Kahl:[51]

Prestige tends to be bestowed through consumption behaviour rather than income. Consumption patterns and interaction networks are intimately linked; people spend their leisure time with others who share their tastes and recreational activities, and they learn new tastes from those with whom they associate.

As a predictor of consumption patterns, social class has long been familiar to the practitioner in marketing, offering market segments which are accessible, measurable and have a discernible life-style. However, the changes which have occurred in the post-war economy have cast doubt upon the reliability of basic socio-economic variables as a guide to consumer habits. That social class is in itself dynamic has been suggested from a variety of sources, giving rise to much theoretical interest and speculation during the 1960s. This outbreak of attention shown towards a variable which had been considered static and clearly defined induced an empirical study into women's shopping behaviour to ascertain the present value of social class and the life cycle as predictive variables.[52] The findings support the viewpoint that social-class distinctions have been obscured by rising incomes and educational levels as suggested by the theoreticians.

The reliability of social class as a predictor was refuted, but at the same time this study did produce positive results showing a relationship between store prestige and social class, confirming an earlier proposition by Martineau.[53]

Although variations in consumption habits between social classes appear to be diminishing, differences are still to be found in shopping ability and methods. Levy's[54] findings show that upper-middle-class women exhibit confidence in their shopping abilities, and are consequently more venturesome in trying out new stores or new products. On the other hand, lower-class housewives are inclined to prefer familiar local outlets for their shopping activities.

Television usage by different social classes was investigated by Levy and Glick,[55] and showed that the 'working-class characteristically "embraced" television, the lower-middle class "accommodated" it, and the upper-middle-class "protested" it'.

Group Influence

Closer and more personalised than social class or culture is the influence exerted upon individual behaviour by the social groups to which he or she belongs. Man, the social animal of Veblen's theories, spends much of his life in group situations, exposed to the norms of his particular social world and motivated to conform to the identity of the group. Conformity, expressed in terms of an individual's willingness to modify information or perception, to fit the stated view of the social group to which he belongs, has been studied most notably by Asch,[56] using experimental conditions.

A laboratory situation was also used by Venkatesan[57] to evaluate the effects of group influence upon individual perception of the quality of men's suits. From this study it was concluded:

> The acceptance of social influence implied that consumers accept information provided by their peer groups on the quality of a product, of a style, etc., which is hard to evaluate objectively. More generally, the group norm or the prevailing group standard directs attention of its members to a new style or a product. It provides a frame of reference which is the first stage in the consumer decision-making process. In many buying situations there exists no objective standard independent of others' opinions.

Stafford[58] undertook a field study with the aim of relating empirically the theories of reference group influence and consumer behaviour. The study produced some interesting pointers to the existence of group influence on brand preferences, together with findings relating brand choice to group cohesiveness and leadership:

> In more cohesive groups, the probability was much higher that the members would prefer the same brand as the group leader.

Conclusions

A further influence upon the purchase decision stems from the business firm itself which may in fact initiate the decision process with its marketing communications (as postulated in Nicosia's model). It is, of course, vital for the marketing practitioner to know the effect his communications programmes have upon the potential users of his products, but this subject is more aptly dealt with under the whole complex area of communications research.

From the empirical testing of the defined influences upon the consumer decision process, it can be clearly seen that whilst some of these variables are already adding depth to the developing theory of consumer behaviour, and at the same time aiding practitioners, others are more resistant to examination. Perception and learning have been shown to be amongst the more fruitful areas of research.

The limited practical application as yet found for such variables as personality, motivation and attitude, though discouraging, is in itself an indication to theoreticians that concepts borrowed from other disciplines will often require some modification. It has been suggested that those factors showing resistance to investigation need to be defined more precisely in terms of the purchase decision. This is a feature of consumer-behaviour theory that exemplifies the benefits to be obtained from the simultaneous and complementary development of theory and practice.

Chapter 5
Communication Theory and Marketing

Introduction

One of the central preoccupations of marketing management concerned with media selection, or in media/advertising research is the development of effective persuasive communications which will successfully accomplish some marketing objective. Unfortunately two of the major problems of marketing management have been to determine which persuasive communications will be most effective, in advance of use, and to measure to what extent the persuasive communication has been successful in achieving its marketing objective. This chapter is addressed to an analysis of the body of theory originating predominantly in social psychology and communications research, which has been applied to the two problems identified here. First, however, a definition.

The use of the phrase 'persuasive communications' reflects in part the evolution of marketing thought which originally saw the task of communicating with the audience as a persuasive function. Members of a target market[1] were persuaded to buy products, and therefore much emphasis was placed on the need to contact each member of the target audience efficiently (hence the rapid and early growth of media-planning activities and techniques).

Persuasive communication, then, in its original sense could be taken to mean all forms of communication from seller to buyer which was aimed at persuading the buyer to buy a product (including advertising, sales promotion, personal selling, packaging, and so on).

Increasingly, however, it has been recognised that the audience plays an active rather than a passive role in the process of persuasive communication. This recognition has lead to emphasis being placed on the activity of 'communication' rather than persuasion, and since communication implies a two-way process, attention has turned to the characteristics of the audience which could mediate the effects of persuasive communication. The audience has become an active seeker of information rather than a passive receiver.

The goals of persuasive communication can be many and varied. Firms, when asked, give a variety of reasons for undertaking advertising, for example increasing brand shares, promoting discounts, introducing new products, and so on. In turn, researchers concerned with the effectiveness of advertising have used a variety of indicators to measure the effectiveness of such activities, including measures of improved consumer disposition, increased awareness and improved attitudes.

Pragmatically, however, most advertisers are interested in the relationship between promotional expenditure and sales. It is this relationship which has proved most difficult to identify. Other elements of the marketing mix often mediate the effects of persuasive communication, for example, pricing, distribution and the nature of the product itself, and it is difficult to control for these in the aggregated form of survey by which most communications effects are measured. Britt[2] makes the point that

> Too many other variables affect the buying decision – price, competition, relative newness of the product and so on – that it is not logical to indicate that sales will be used as the measure of advertising effectiveness. . . . In rare instances it has been found possible to relate advertising and communications goals to sales by a strict control of extraneous variables such as price and point of purchase efforts. But without controlled experimentation, a direct cause and effect relationship between advertising and sales cannot be accepted as a defensible proof of advertising.

Underlying the problem of measurement of promotional effectiveness is the level of understanding of the fundamental processes involved. Survey data gathered on a cross-sectional basis, or experimental data gathered under the restrictive conditions of the experiment, have not been able to explain adequately why certain promotional campaigns are effective and others are not. For example, does increased awareness through advertising exposure precede purchasing behaviour, or does the consumer having made his or her choice then deliberately seek out information which supports his or her decision?[3]

Increasing recognition of conceptual problems such as this has led to an increasing concern among marketing theoreticians with the communications process. This chapter will review theories of communication behaviour, which have been developed in the marketing context, which have sought to view the consumer from a socio-psychological perspective. Such theories have as their aim the enrichment of marketing's understanding of the process and effects of persuasive communication.

The chapter is split into two sections. The first section discusses an early model of communication, the stimulus–response model, and a subsequent marketing derivation, the 'hierarchy of effects' concept. Some of the problems of this interpretation of the effects of communication are discussed, and the section then continues by discussing three distinct research traditions from the behavioural sciences which have provided fundamental inputs for the subsequent development of models of marketing communication.

The second section reviews some of the important models of marketing communication which have emerged from the application of these concepts from the behavioural sciences. As such it focuses on the development of marketing communication theory. The number of reported applications in this area is relatively large and only a few examples are picked out to illustrate the main lines of development.

AN EARLY MODEL OF THE COMMUNICATION PROCESS

Much of the early work into the effects of persuasive communication was derived from the 'stimulus–response' theory of learning. Advertisements were considered to be stimuli which elicited some form of response. Consequently, adopting the findings of psychologists who had looked at the phenomenon in experimental conditions, it was argued that purchasing could be regarded as a form of learned behaviour in response to certain stimuli – the stronger the stimulus–response connection, the more likely purchasing behaviour would be in response to advertisements. Such an interpretation led to an early and intense effort among practitioners to find methods which maximised the target market's exposure to the stimuli of advertisements, within certain cost limits (that is, the growth and development of media-planning techniques).

Recognising, however, that the audience, even when 'hit' by stimuli, did not respond by purchasing, the idea of a 'gradient' of response was evolved.

Briefly, it was argued that certain activities must logically precede the act of purchase itself, and that the purpose of advertising might well be to push consumers up the steps of this 'gradient' until they eventually purchased. Thus, Lavidge and Steiner[4] proposed that advertising could be thought of as a force which must move people up a series of steps. They suggest:

1. Near the bottom of the steps stand potential purchasers who are completely unaware of the existence of the product or service in question.
2. Closer to purchasing, but still a long way from the cash register, are those who are merely aware of its existence.
3. Up a step are prospects who know what a product has to offer.
4. Still closer to purchasing are those who have favourable attitudes toward the product – those who like the product.
5. Those whose favourable attitudes have developed to the point of preference are up still another step.
6. Even closer to purchasing are consumers who couple preference with a desire to buy and the conviction that the purchase would be wise.
7. Finally, of course, is the step which translates this attitude into actual purchase.

Lavidge and Steiner's conceptual foundation is strongly aligned with the tradition of research on the adoption and diffusion of agricultural innovations.[5] (See Chapter 7 for a review of the application of this research tradition to the marketing context.) Their 'hierarchy of effects' model, as it became known, influenced many successive attempts to measure advertising effectiveness as it suggested a means for setting communications objectives in terms of moving consumers from point to point up a scale of increasing probability of purchase.

However, one of the main problems of their model is that it presupposes that there are distinct stages in this sequence and that, in particular, attitude change precedes purchasing behaviour. As the introduction to this chapter suggests, this may not necessarily be the case.

From the practitioner's point of view there were two problems in applying this concept. First, how were each of the stages to be identified? Most of the early criticisms of the 'hierarchy' model were based on criticisms of the methodological soundness of the research methods used to determine the effectiveness of an advertisement in bringing about awareness, recall, attitude change, and so on. Pollit provides a listing of some of the measurement techniques which have become associated with these 'hierarchy of effects' models. His main conclusion is that

> The main problems that arose from the use of all the measurements, despite their essentially common sense origins, have been that they have produced results which have been very difficult to reconcile with any reasonable judgement expectations about particular advertisements and campaigns. They did not provide common sense answers.[6]

The second and more fundamental problem is that Lavidge and Steiner's model assumes that attitude change precedes behavioural change. This problem has not been satisfactorily resolved. Moscovici had identified this problem:

> A causal relationship and a 'meaning' relationship between attitude and behaviour can be distinguished. When attitude is changed first, the aim is to cause change in behaviour. On the other hand, if behaviour changes first, a change in attitude is involved and serves to give a meaning to the already achieved behaviour. Attitude may thus be viewed either as a mechanism directing behaviour or as a modality which confers on behaviour its meaning.[7]

These early 'stimulus–response' models of the way in which persuasive communication works assume a passive, subordinate role for the audience. However, increasingly it had become evident to marketing practitioners that the audience itself operated as a mediating factor on the effects of communication. In order to understand these mediating effects attention was increasingly focused on the findings of three distinct research traditions.

THREE RESEARCH TRADITIONS

(a) The Role of Personal Influence

In the early 1950s at Columbia University in the United States Katz and Lazarsfeld[8] were responsible for a programme of research which dealt extensively with the relationship between people and the mass communications to which they were exposed.

Based on their observations of voting patterns in the 1940 presidential elections, their programme focused specifically on the importance of informal (that is not commercially sponsored) channels of communication. Their results gave rise to the concepts of (1) a 'two-step flow of communication', and (2) opinion leadership.

The 'two-step flow of communication' concept suggests that information from commercially sponsored sources tends to be sought out only by certain members of any 'target' audience. They in turn will pass on this information to the rest of the population, who will rely on these few 'opinion leaders' for advice and opinion.

The authors summarise this succinctly in their review of a study of the adoption of a new drug among physicians: 'It may be useful to think of the structure of social and professional relations among physicians in a community as a network of communication, through which information, influence and innovation flow.'[9]

The marketing implications of their work were obvious, and much attention has been devoted in marketing to understanding patterns of interpersonal communication and, in particular, the characteristics of the opinion leader. This work is reviewed below.

(b) Diffusion of Innovation

The second distinct research tradition is that of the rural sociologist's study of the diffusion of agricultural innovation.

This research area dates back to the early 1920s in the United States, when administrators in the United States Department of Agriculture Federal Extension Service instigated an evaluation of their programme's effectiveness. Much of the important work in this area stems from the Ryan and Gross[10] investigation of the diffusion of hybrid seed corn.

One of the major findings of their work (subsequently replicated by other researchers) related to the use of different sources of information at different stages in the adoption process.

Reference has already been made to the adoption process in connection with 'hierarchy of effects' models. The adoption-process model was based on the findings of many individual research findings[11] which suggested that the adoption of innovation could be seen as a process with five stages: awareness, interest, evaluation, trial and adoption.

Ryan and Gross found that at the early stages of buying new products, when the buyer was not committed to buying any particular innovation, he tended to use basically formal sources of information (commercial sources). However, as he increasingly became more committed to purchasing the new product, that is evaluating the new product in terms of its suitability for his own requirements, then he tended to turn to informal personal sources of information (such as friends and neighbours).

A second generalisation of their work was that early adopters of innovation tended to prefer using relatively formal channels of information throughout the adoption process since, by definition, there were relatively few people to ask advice from who had experience of the product. By comparison, later adopters tended to rely more heavily on interpersonal communication.

The rural sociologists also developed a series of generalisations about the characteristics of the opinion leader. These were subsequently developed in a specific marketing context and are reviewed below.

The two research traditions thus far reviewed show considerable overlap, both in their areas of interest and in the methodology adopted. Both discussed the relative importance of different sources of information in the process of adoption of new products, and both emphasised that the spread of information on new products and services should be viewed from a sociological perspective.

Their research methodology, too, was similar. Both used a form of field survey which sought to exclude random variations in the information they collected by statistical control.

The third research tradition from which models of communication have emerged is that of communications research. This tradition was based extensively on data gathered by experimental techniques by Hovland and his associates at Yale University in the immediate post-war period.

(c) Communication and Persuasion

Increasing dissatisfaction with the early 'stimulus–response' model of communication reviewed above leads to the development of what might be termed a 'phenomenistic' approach to understanding communication processes. Researchers such as Schramm,[12] Bauer,[13] and Klapper[14] were among the first to propose that communication could only be understood as a transaction, with the audience taking an active rather than a passive role.

Adopting this perspective, communication (and hence the success or failure of persuasive communication) can only be understood by focusing on the individual predispositions, social influences, personal experiences and other factors which people bring to communication situations. Such an approach emphasises that the media are operating as only one influence in many on individual behaviour.

Early work in this research tradition was focused around four major areas: the source of communication, the message, the channels of information through which the message passes and the receiver or audience.

Experimental evidence showed that the credibility of the source of information can modify the effectiveness of persuasive communication. Hovland, Janis and Kelley[15] identified two components of source credibility: (1) 'expertness', or the extent to which the source is considered capable of making valid assertions; and (2) 'trustworthiness', or the extent to which the audience is confident in the sources actually making such valid assertions.

The authors' work showed that, *under experimental conditions*, immediate attitude change in the direction advocated by the communication was most pronounced for the high credibility source and least pronounced for the low credibility source. A follow-up measure of attitude change administered three weeks after the presentation indicated that the differences originally present had disappeared. In other words, the value of the high credibility of the source diminished over time.

The same researchers also showed that the communication or 'message' itself could influence the reception of persuasive communication. In particular, attention was focused on the effects of order of presentation of argument, of irrational versus rational appeals, and of fear appeals. Their results demonstrated that, depending on the characteristics of the audience, different forms of presentation of a persuasive communication or 'message' would have differing effects. The phrase 'depending on the characteristics of the audience' is crucially important in any interpretation of the findings of their results. Subsequently, applications of these findings in a marketing context have often failed to make this qualification.

Channels of communication have been studied in detail by Klapper.[16] Findings in this area relate predominantly to the use of relatively formal channels of communication, namely qualitative differences between the various mass media. Generalisations which emerge from these findings are relatively scarce since most conclusions are situation-specific. As Klapper states: 'Considerable research on the relative persuasive power of the several media bears out the widespread belief that they are in fact differentially persuasive. Although some generalisations may be hesitantly drawn, the data more clearly indicate that the relative powers of the media differ markedly from one persuasive task to another.'

One interesting line of enquiry, however, has been the analysis of the credibility of the channels of information themselves. Fuchs[17] reports a study in which there were found to be distinct 'source' effects in the media used to convey persuasive communication. Such intermediary source effects indicated possible ways of conceptualising and ultimately measuring so-called 'qualitative differences' between different media vehicles. (Advertising media are frequently selected on the grounds of 'impact', 'power', 'atmosphere' or 'immediacy' and 'quality of presentation'. These are essentially subjective judgements on the part of the media planner, and form the basis of 'qualitative' differences between various media.)

Finally, much attention has been focused on the characteristics of the audience as they affect reception of persuasive communication. Sociologists such as Katz and Lazarsfeld[18] had emphasised the importance of personal influence in modifying the effects of mass communication. Psychologists, on the other hand, were beginning to look at the importance of personality, ability and message variables in the effects of communication.

Hovland, Janis and Kelley[19] found that the I.Q. of the receiver, his motivations at a given time and the responses he had learned were likely to influence the reception of persuasive communication, and that these factors reacted specifically with message characteristics, like source, appeals and form of content.

Understanding of the process and effects of mass communication developed throughout the 1950s, and, particularly in the United States, marketing practitioners in a search for relative competitive advantage began to use and develop these concepts.

One of the most important contributions of this third research tradition to subsequent marketing thought was growing concern with the need to consider the communications process as an interactive system, where in order for a persuasive communication to be successful, all elements of the process had to be taken into account.

Klapper[20] provided a summary of this position in 1960:

1. Mass communication ordinarily does not serve as a necessary and sufficient cause of audience effects, but rather functions among and through a nexus of mediating factors and influences.
2. These mediating factors are such that they typically render mass communication a contributory agent, but not the sole cause, in a process of reinforcing the existing conditions. . . . Regardless of whether the effect in question be social or individual, the media are more likely to reinforce than to change.
3. On such occasions as mass communication does function in the service of change . . . either
    (a) The mediating factors will be found to be inoperative and the effect of the media direct, or
    (b) The mediating factors that normally favour reinforcement will be found themselves impelling toward change.

4. There are certain residual situations in which mass communication seems to produce direct effect or directly and of itself to serve certain psycho-physical functions.

5. The efficacy of mass communication, either as a contributory agent or as an agent of direct effect, is affected by various aspects of the media and communication themselves or of the communication situation.

Klapper's comments summarise some of the main conclusions of the work in sociology and psychology which underpins much of the subsequent development of theory concerning marketing communication. As such the preceding review is necessarily brief. Interested readers are recommended to refer to the major texts referenced.

Attention now turns to the development of these concepts in terms of marketing communications theory; in other words, to the interchange between basic behavioural research into the processes of human communication and the applications of findings to consumer and advertising problems.

Many people have worked in both areas (notably Lazarsfeld), providing benefits of cross-stimulation for both scientific understanding and practical application. The rest of this chapter provides a brief description of some of the main contributions which models of communication have made to marketing theory.

MODELS OF MARKETING COMMUNICATION

Opinion Leadership

One of the most well-documented applications of communications theory in the marketing context has been the development of Katz and Lazarsfeld's model of personal influence. There are, it is suggested, certain individuals within any social system who are used as a source of information and opinion by other members of the social system. Such individuals wield a degree of personal influence, or an ability to cause a change in an individual's attitude or behaviour as a result of interpersonal communication.

The 'two-step flow of communication' concept suggests that

information and hence influence flows from the mass media to the opinion leader and so to his followers. This 'two-step flow' concept has subsequently been revised as it has been recognised that the opinion leader may be the recipient of enquiries on some issues, and initiate enquiries on others. King and Summers,[21] in a study of fashion diffusion, found that 39 per cent of those engaged in interpersonal communication mentioned participation both as a transmitter and as a receiver of information.

Marketing has traditionally emphasised the need to reach influentials in any promotional process, but these were generally defined by high occupational status or participation in the community. But one of the important contributions of Katz and Lazarsfeld's work was in pointing out that people are most often influenced by those with whom they are in *everyday* contact.

Increasingly in the early 1960s attention was turned to identifying the characteristics of such opinion leaders. Rogers[22] had suggested in a review based primarily on the findings of rural sociology that opinion leaders evidence more social participation than followers, although the former are 'not necessarily the power holders or the formal leaders of their community'; they also appear to be more cosmopolitan than followers, that is more orientated outside their communities. By definition, opinion leaders are 'usually supernormative members' and 'especially familiar with and loyal to group standards and values'.[23]

Unfortunately, however, it has proved difficult to identify any specific profile of opinion-leader traits as Table 5.1 shows. Since standardised traits are difficult to identify, marketing's attention

TABLE 5.1 *Summary profile of opinion-leader traits*

Characteristic	Findings
Age	Varies by product category
Social status	Generally same as advisee
Gregariousness	High
Cosmopolitanism	Limited evidence that higher than advisee
Knowledge	Generally greater for area of influence
Personality	No major distinguishing traits
Norm adherence	Generally greater than advisees
Innovativeness	Higher than advisees

SOURCE: T. S. Robertson, *Innovative Behavior and Communication* (New York: Holt, Rinehart & Winston, 1971).

has been turned to the examination of certain situational factors, for specific product categories and within certain product categories it may well eventually be possible to identify general opinion-leadership profiles.[24]

Katz and Lazarsfeld[25] and, later, Rogers[26] have all concluded that opinion leaders make greater use of the mass media. Such a finding would have important implications if it could be replicated in a marketing context. Unfortunately such replications are few.

Given that the characteristics of the opinion leader for a specific product category could be identified, it would then be feasible to appeal directly to the opinion leader, or as Mancuso[27] suggests, create opinion leaders for new products. One of the fundamental problems in the first approach is that media-profile data are usually collected on the basis of socio-economic classifications, and that unless the opinion leader could be described in these terms, evolving the most appropriate media-mix to take advantage of this phenomenon is impracticable.

Information and Perceived Risk

Early research into the diffusion of innovation showed that various channels of communication were preferred at different stages in the adoption of new agricultural products. This work was subsequently replicated in both consumer and industrial marketing contexts.[28] It was found that buyers at the early stages of buying a new product tended to use relatively formal sources of information, that is via the 'mass' media, whereas at the later stages of evaluation and adoption they tended to use relatively informal sources of information, namely interpersonal communication.

Such evidence suggested that a firm's ability to influence the adoption of new products through the mass media is relatively limited. The role of the mass media seemed to be to create initial awareness and provide information rather than to create behavioural change.

Conscious of this problem, researchers began to look at the reasons for preference of informal sources of information at later stages in the adoption process. Bauer had suggested that this was a function of the level of risk perceived in making a particular decision: 'The amount and nature of perceived risk will define consumer information needs, and consumers will seek out sources and types of information to reduce this.'[29]

Subsequent authors[30] have shown that in some instances the information provided by the commercial source through formal channels of communication is sufficient. However, as the risk perceived in purchasing increases, it is likely that the buyer will seek additional information from others with experience of the product who may be seen as more objective and trustworthy than commercial sources.

From a marketing perspective it would therefore seem important to define those areas where the level of perceived risk in adopting the action advocated by the persuasive communication is high. These are the areas where, by definition, opinion leadership and personal influence may be highest. Day reports a study which has looked at the relationship between media and word of mouth:

> Advertising was found to play an essential role in the acceptance of a new and an established brand of a convenience food product. Very simply, the role of advertising was to provide the preconditions for success, which for the new brand was primarily to build awareness and for the established brand was to maintain existing favourable attitudes. In both cases ultimate success, in terms of creating and reinforcing favourable attitudes, largely rested with the ability of the brand to generate favourable word of mouth communications and to provide a satisfactory usage experience.[31]

Message Effects

The type of message itself, its organisation and the nature of its appeal, had been shown experimentally to have an effect on the success or failure of persuasive communication. Very little research evidence is available, however, to show that the effects of message attributes has been applied to a marketing context.

The exception to this generalisation is research which has looked at the nature of threat/fear appeals. These can be categorised as messages alluding to unfavourable consequences which will occur from failure to follow the communicator's recommendations. An example of such a fear appeal would be a public-health campaign.

One of the best-known experiments in this area is that cited by Janis and Feshbach.[32] Their main conclusion was that a strong fear appeal was less effective than either moderate or mild fear appeals in producing a positive attitude to dental hygiene.

More recent research on fear appeals has tended to suggest that neither extremely strong nor very weak appeals are most effective.[33] Ray and Wilkie[34] suggest that marketing's emphasis has been focused predominantly on the Janis and Feshbach study, which suggests that the more fear the less effect, and has ignored behavioural research findings which indicate that fear produces some effects which facilitate the reception of a communicator's recommendations (where fear may heighten drive thus leading to greater attention and interest in the message than if no drive were aroused).

At the beginning of this chapter it was stated that the purpose of marketing communication was to elicit some form of action, and considerable fear research on 'action' has been conducted. Concepts derived from experimental settings have been used to induce people to get tetanus injections, improve dental practices, see their doctor, stop smoking and take chest X-rays.[35]

There is little evidence, however, to show the effects of fear appeals in a commercially sponsored setting. Considerations of ethics would probably preclude publication of findings on such effects, even if such methods had been adopted.

MODELS OF INFORMATION PROCESSING

Increasing concern has been expressed by marketing practitioners with the efficiency of different approaches to packaging, pricing, advertising themes, layouts, and so on. Better promotional decisions have become a source of competitive advantage, and this has led to increased emphasis being placed on techniques of measuring advertising effectiveness.

Early attempts to measure the effectiveness of advertising stressed the stimulus–response model of advertising response. Consequently the first advertising researchers studied the Ebinghaus[36] research on memory and applied laboratory techniques of experimentation to reading actual advertisements. Attention was focused on the problems of how big should the advertisement be and how frequently should the respondent be exposed to it – the key dependent variable in such studies being 'recall'.[37]

The problem with such techniques, however, is that attention and recognition attracted by technical ability does not necessarily lead to effective persuasion for the product or service advertised. Thus the measurement of the effects or actions resulting from advertising has increasingly become a major preoccupation of marketing practitioners. However, simple generalisable models are difficult to evolve from aggregated survey or panel data, and, consequently, emphasis has been placed on the understanding of communications systems based on an analysis of the processes at work.

Communications researchers have long emphasised that the system through which the individual receives his or her information should be the focus of study, where each part is treated as interacting with the whole (see above). Increasingly marketing researchers have adopted this concept and are beginning to consider the effects of commercially orientated communications, not in isolation, but in the context of the receiver's relationship with his or her environment, past experience with the source, particular problems and needs, and so on. This has led to the development of so-called micro simulations of consumer behaviour.

Adopting this approach, a descriptive model can be built up of all the influences on the consumer in the market-place, using many of the concepts originating in sociology and psychology already discussed, pulling together the main components of the communications process. Then the effects of changes in any one factor are measured by using the model as a working analogy of the real system.

Repeated simulations of the model are used to gradually build up a 'history' of results of the effect of changes in any number of influencing factors.

Claychamp and Amstutz[38] report a study of such a simulation in the ethical pharmaceuticals market. The simulation looks at the interaction of patients with individual histories of treatments and complaints with doctors, each of whom has memories of past drug effectiveness, and attitudes determined partly by controllable marketing variables (for example advertising, direct mail, representatives).

Such simulations, grounded in the findings of sociology and psychology, offer one of the most promising potential methods of measuring the effects of variations in the promotional mix.

SUMMARY

This chapter has prescribed a brief review of some of the major developments in marketing communications theory which have been applied to practical business problems. In particular it has focused on developments which are beginning to provide answers to the following communications problems.

(a) What is the role of information (from persuasive communication) before purchase of a product takes place?

(b) What determines the level of response to persuasive communication?

(c) Which channels of communication (media) are most effective, and why?

(d) Which form of message presentation is most effective?

(e) How to derive a general conceptual framework for understanding the effects of variations in the promotional mix.

In doing so, marketing is moving towards the establishment of its own body of theory in the area of the process and effects of persuasive communication. It has abstracted itself from the behavioural sciences in which the original communications concepts were based, has begun to establish its own typologies, and generalisations are beginning to emerge from these which are increasingly being applied to practical marketing problems.

Chapter 6

Channels of Distribution

THE ACT OF EXCHANGE

The term 'channel of distribution' generally requires supplementation in order to limit the meaning of the word to the type of activity or item being considered. In a commercial sense, the term 'distribution' covers the act and process of disposing, or sharing, commodities, so that they may yield benefits, or be made ready to yield benefits to those who give value for them. The salesman uses the term to refer to the wholesaler or the retailer who sells the type of merchandise he has to offer. The economist is concerned with 'the distribution of the National Income among the various agents of production, in accordance with the quantity of each several agent, and the services which it renders'[1]. In his examination of distribution in this sense, Marshall linked the process of distribution with the act of exchange which brings together these 'agents of production'. This act of exchange is central to the distribution process.

Exchange involves two entities, whose interest may be different but who hope to gain from the exchange which is made. In order that the exchange may take place, however, both parties must agree that the items exchanged, usually goods and money, are equal in value, and until that agreement is reached no exchange will take place, a matter which reflects the need for market knowledge, as well as the need for a free flow of information concerning the market.

In commerce, the exchange is made with a view to some subsequent action which will have the effect of bringing the hoped-for gain from the transaction, and this subsequent action has been referred to as a 'transformation'.[2] The transformation effectively adds utility to the commodity, a utility which may lead to a second exchange when advantage may be taken of a different supply and demand situation. The utilities or satisfactions to be added to the commodity can be shown as follows:

(1) *Form* – the commodity is changed in shape or form. This process frequently separates the distribution of the primary products of agriculture, mining, and fishing from the distribution of manufactured goods;

(2) *Place* – the location of the commodity is changed so that it becomes available in a different market;

(3) *Time* – the commodity is stored until the supply/demand situation gives a new and higher value, or in order to manage the supply situation; and

(4) *Assortment* – the product is sorted into homogeneous classes to enable customers to buy only those classes they want, or into heterogeneous classes to allow the customer to make many purchases in one location, thus reducing the cost of the exchange.[3]

Transaction Costs

The act of negotiating an exchange calls for some effort or cost as buyer and seller search among all the alternatives available in the market. Most of the searching is done by the buyer, as in the consumer-goods market, but sellers must spend resources maintaining a profile in the market-place.

The costs are not all easily calculated in value terms so far as the household customer is concerned, for both physical and psychological costs are involved.

In an isolated purchase, the buyer will continue to search until it is felt that further expenditure on searching will not produce any increased benefit, that is until the increased benefit is marginal. In a repeat-purchase situation the buyer will try to reduce the cost of the transaction in two ways. First he will reduce the number of alternatives he is willing to examine, to the point where he only considers one, so long as the market is stable. Second, the actual transaction will be routinised by mutual agreement to a set of rules for procurement and payment of supplies. Performance on each side rests on the belief that the other party will behave as expected.[4] Advertising serves to routinise the specifying of a commodity by making the brand name stand in place of a specification.

Sequential Exchanges

A channel of distribution can now be described as a sequence of transactions, each of which is undertaken for the purpose of adding utility in a subsequent transformation process. The possibility of intermediaries being inserted between the prime producer and the final consumer was explored by Alderson and Martin[5] who concluded that the number of intermediaries could be increased so long as each additional transaction is optimal in that it is preferred to any available alternative. A sequence of transactions has reached its optimum when costs cannot be decreased by increasing or decreasing the number of transations

A channel of distribution therefore consists of that set of business entities which perform all the functions utilised to move a product and its title from producer to consumer.[6] The arrangements between the business entities include not only the price of the merchandise but also the services which will be given in passing the goods and their title, expectations as to future transactions, and agreements regarding transactions method and costs. Bucklin's definition excludes the addition of form utility, and avoids the difficulty of describing channels which include assembly operations in which different transactions channels merge in manufacturing entities. In this definition, when a change is made in the product, the channel ends and a new one begins. It enables the final purchaser to be included, thus completing the system, since the product is only changed when consumed.

The entities normally considered in the channel therefore consist of the following:

The manufacturer;
The intermediaries – wholesaler, retailer, transport and storage specialists, selling agents, factors;
The customer – household purchasing agent, industrial purchaser, consumer.

In the case of a primary product, the channel would consist of the following:

The producer – farmer, forester, fisherman, miner;

An alternative is to use 'sales per person engaged', and this was done by Pollard and Hughes,[11] who concluded that sales per person engaged increased with the sales size of the establishment, thus confirming Marshall's view. A more rigorous study by George and Hill[12] examined labour-productivity changes in distribution in the period 1961–6. They were interested in establishing causes of the changes, and once again confirmed the effect of increasing sales size using the same measures. They suggested that, as sales increased, opportunities were created for shop owners to utilise their existing staff and plant more efficiently through increasing the capital investment and applying technical and organisational knowledge (T.O.K.). For all types of trade, they were able to establish that 60 per cent of the improvement was due to increased capital intensity and 40 per cent to the application of T.O.K. In a sectional analysis, differences could be identified between different forms of organisation, and different types of trade, with, for example, all the gains in labour productivity by co-operatives being attributed to increased capital intensity. Not unexpectedly, they found that the best investment for improving labour productivity, apart from new premises, was in converting to self-service, while extending the existing premises was only half as effective.

Labour productivity became a matter of importance in the 1960s when the government felt that too many people were being employed in the service industries, and led to the Selective Employment Tax on those industries to squeeze out 'surplus' labour. The effects of this were investigated by Reddaway.[13]

Competition in Retailing

The classical economists seemed unable to agree whether a large number of shops would result in waste to be passed on to the consumer in prices, or in competition which would improve efficiency and therefore reduce prices. The nature of the competitive situation had always been recognised as 'peculiar',[14] a characteristic sometimes attributed to the irrational nature of the shopper, but more accurately to the conditions of location monopoly, as Chamberlin pointed out.[15] In his critique of capitalism (*Capitalism, Socialism and Democracy*, 1942), Schumpeter suggested that 'the competition that matters arises not from additional shops of the same type, but of different types'. By this he meant that alternative monopoly powers could be obtained through the acquisition of agency rights, a licence to retail certain commodities such as beer, through the use of lower-than-average prices on some or all of the merchandise, or the provision of extra incentives to use a particular shop. These advantages had the effect of attracting customers for short periods from the monopolist location, and therefore of eroding that monopoly.

McNair[16] recognised the oligopolistic situation in his 'wheel of retailing' concept in which the retailer is in the position described by the 'kinked demand curve' model, where prices have stabilised and he can neither increase nor reduce his prices. He can only reduce prices if he is sure other retailers will not follow him. He resorts to non-price attractions which others imitate at a cost, until all feel compelled to raise prices. With each upward jerk, the trade becomes increasingly vulnerable to new entrants using price competition incorporating a 'stripped-down' form of merchandising or some cost-saving techniques. As these new entrants increase in number, the share of market available to each one also stabilises, and the price-stabilising forces reflected in the kinked demand curve reappear to complete the turn of the wheel.

Concentration

Retailers have options available to them to reduce the level of competition in that they can acquire their competitors, or merge with them, or they can make agreements to co-operate with them. Agreements to restrict competition are, of course, subject to the provisions of the Monopolies and Restrictive Practices Act, and, to date, no agreements of this type between retailers have received approval. Acquisition and merger brings with it the benefits of large-scale production which enable more attractive offers to be made, and in a densely populated island like the United Kingdom, it is possible for a multiple retailer to supervise a very large number of outlets in order to achieve national coverage and to reap further economies in advertising and the transference of loyalty. In more thinly populated countries, the achievement of national coverage is more difficult and multiples tend to have a regional basis of operation. Comparative data on the retail trades in the Common Market[17] provide the levels of concentration which are shown in Table 6.1.

TABLE 6.1 *Shares of retail trade*

Country	Share of twenty-five largest firms (per cent)
France	16·5
West Germany	19·0
United Kingdom	29·8

In the United States, Bucklin[18] noted that nationally the top thirty-five retailers accounted for only 12·4 per cent of retail sales in 1970, while in the 218 metropolitan areas, the top four food retailers held an average 50 per cent of the market in 1963.

Contrasting national levels of concentration in retailing with levels of concentration in manufacturing, Bucklin found that retail levels were very much lower. Similarly, Metcalf[19] found that food manufacturers tend to be more concentrated than retailers. The three largest manufacturing units accounted for 35 per cent of the output in the United Kingdom.

Factors which explained the level of concentration to some extent were income levels and population density, historical and institutional factors and the presence of an import centre. As economic growth brings rising incomes and greater population density, the degree of concentration would be likely to increase. In some areas, factors such as the co-op movement and the development of self-service have acted to increase the level of concentration. In other areas which are served by large ports, multiples can obtain economies in handling imported foods, providing an incentive to operate from the port.

Barriers to Entry

Another means of limiting competition is to attempt to raise barriers which prospective new entrants to the industry will find difficult to surmount. Customarily, three main types of barrier are distinguished: First is the preference of buyers for the goods and services offered by existing firms; second is the absolute cost advantage which an existing firm may have over potential entrants; and third is the economy of scale which may be enjoyed by existing firms by virtue of their size. A possible fourth group of legal barriers, such as the need to hold a licence for a particular type of trade, a franchise for a particular brand of merchandise, planning permission, or certificates of competence or health, might also be considered if the restrictions could not be fitted into the customary categories.

Behind this barrier, existing firms will reap a monopoly profit which can be related to the size of the barrier. If the profit they reap is greater than can be justified by the barrier to entry, they will attract new entrants. Potential entrants, too, may see opportunities to reduce costs once over the barrier to a level lower than the average, as in McNair's 'wheel of retailing', but they must also anticipate the response of existing firms to their entry. The responses of existing firms to an innovation were explored by McCammon[20] who suggested eight hypotheses towards the response resulting in a change. One of these proposes that a firm will respond incrementally to innovation unless its core market is threatened. In that case the response to innovation will proceed quickly.

The level of the barrier to entry varies with the type of merchandise, but McAnally[21] suggests that barriers generally are higher now than formerly, mentioning plant costs, staff training and wages levels, planning laws and local-authority control.

Retail Policies

From the retailer's point of view, policies are required in respect of any one shop location which will solve the problems of creating an attractiveness function to overcome the deterrence function of distance and competition. The attractiveness function consists of the assortment of goods, prices and services, as well as the ambience of the shop. The function of attraction is to draw customers from as close to competing centres as possible, and from the shops in the centre who are in competition. The communication of policy in creating attractiveness was at one time a simple matter of window display, but now requires the services of other media since inter-centre competition increases with affluence.

The location problem was first approached by Reilly[22] using a static model which he verbalised as follows: 'Two towns will

attract trade from any intermediate point in direct proportion
to the population of the respective towns, and in inverse proportion to the square of the distance that the intermediate point
is from either town.'

Subsequently expressed in the form of an equation by
Converse,[23] Huff,[24] and Lakshmanan and Hansen,[25] the model
was extended to include every likely competing shopping centre
and every definable aggregation of population and its spending
power, to produce a computer-orientated predictive model of
the following form:

$$S_j = \sum_{i=1}^{m} C_i \frac{F_j^{\beta} \, d_{ij}^{a}}{\sum\limits_{k=1}^{n} F_k^{\beta} \, d_{ik}^{a}},$$

where

S_j = sales in the jth centre of a series of n centres;

C_i = consumer/retail spending power available in the ith
zone of n zones;

F_j = the size (shopping-floor space) or attractive power of
the shopping centre in the jth zone;

F_k = the size or attractive power of the shopping centre in
the kth zone;

d_{ij} = the driving time between the centroids of zone i and
centre j;

β = an exponent applied to F, the attractive power of the
centre;

a = an exponent applied to d;

m = the total number of zones of spending power, and

n = the total number of shopping centres considered.

This approach was adopted by most planners in the United
Kingdom, often with disastrous results since it was based on a
static concept, and the idea that the sole attractiveness-function
component was shopping space.

Geographers in the United Kingdom took a different line,
and used survey methods to identify catchment areas and the
differences and similarities between shopping centres. This
resulted in the development of a system for classifying centres
and relating that classification to the expected limits of the

catchment area. An early study on these lines was that of Thorpe and Rhodes[26] with later studies exploring the travel behaviour and allocation of expenditure behaviour.

Market researchers who became involved with the problems of multiple retailers in estimating what sales ought to be made in existing shops, or what they might be in a proposed shop, tended to build models based on survey material. Starting with an assumption that sales are a function of a number of independent variables which may also be interrelated, they consulted the retailers' opinions as to what these might be, thus allowing other attracting factors than shopping-floor space to be included in the equation, measured them, and then using a battery of multiple-regression techniques, produced a model which appeared to explain sales in terms of the specific variables. Prominent in this approach has been Heald of Gallup Ltd.[27]

Although this appeared a satisfactory method of including more components of the attractiveness function, it does not readily manage the different motivations of customers, for if the retailer had been of the opinion that the range of his assortment was important to customers, whereas in reality his customer were really motivated by price, the model may not be quite so useful. The best that could be done in such a model was to disaggregate the catchment area population by socio-economic groupings, each of which could be identified as being attracted in varying proportions to that particular type of shop. Work on shopper types had already been done by Greeno, Sommers, and Kernan[28] in 1973 in the United States, and Lunn[29] and Beazley[30] in the United Kingdom in which both a trait-theory and a self-theory approach was made to identifying personality traits and their associated shopping behaviour. The problem of introducing personality traits into such a model when it is difficult to measure their presence in the population was tackled by Thabor[31] when he constructed a model for a French retail-wine multiple. In this case he identified the only personality trait he was interested in, price consciousness, and ignored the remainder.

This type of research promises assistance to retailers who are reshaping their policies in line with the changing aspirations and changing shopping behaviour of their existing customers, their sons and daughters. It also provides an exhaustive method for designing a new type of store which will allow new entrants to mount the entry barriers to the retail field.

Retail Operations

In the process of putting policies into practice, the retailer is faced with the need to allocate his resources in such a way as to maximise the total yield. The allocation problem is common to all input–output situations where there are many inputs. For the retailer these inputs are the shelf space which is subject to constraint, the assortment of merchandise, labour, customer services and advertising.

Studies of shelf space are mainly orientated to supermarkets and self-service stores where space is treated as a resource to be allocated to merchandise assortments. Labour in this situation tends to be mainly non-selling and can be reduced to a cost of handling, allowing several of the resources allocated to be optimised simultaneously to give the best proportion of each stock item in the assortment, and therefore to determine the department, counter or shelf space to be allocated to each item for the purpose of maximising sales or profits. The problem here is that prices realisable are not the same in every shop of a multiple since competitive pressures differ from one location to another.

Many of the studies[32] have their origin in the United States beginning in 1929 with the U.S. Department of Commerce Study conducted by Wroe Alderson to determine product net margins. The 1950s saw the beginning of serious efforts to relate shelf-space allocations to sales and to profits, with some studies sponsored by the U.S. Department of Agriculture, and others by the National Cash Register Company (N.C.R.), grocery multiples and academics. In Europe, the Cooperative College in England and the Universities of Cologne and Frankfurt were engaged in similar studies.

The Wholesale Trade: its Functions

The public attitude to the role performed by wholesalers of all kinds reflects the common desire to cut out the middleman, and to obtain wholesale prices. Often regarded as unnecessary, or unproductive, it remains commercially obvious that were the trade not fulfilling a function in the distribution channels, it would be unable to exist.

The theoretical rationale for its presence in adding utility to the product has already been demonstrated by Alderson and Martin.[33] Bucklin[34] examined the theoretical base for the stock-holding wholesaler and suggested that stockholding fulfils the function of isolating the risks associated with title to goods, thus allowing manufacturers to reduce manufacturing costs, and customers to have a shorter delivery time. Where no stocks are held by intermediaries, manufacturing costs will tend to rise and delivery time to lengthen.

This is a full list of the functions performed by wholesalers of all types.

Minimising total transactions.[35] The total number of contacts required in a system is smaller when an intermediary is used. The intermediary may also achieve economies of scale through having a larger assortment of information 'bits'.

If no intermediary is available, the customer's time available to each manufacturer would be reduced thus limiting the marketing opportunities of the industry, as in the case of the pharmaceutical industry whose detail men have difficulty in obtaining time from doctors.

Minimising the system of stockholding costs.[36] Where stocks require to be carried at many retail points, the wholesaler may, by massing the reserve stocks, reduce the ratio of stocks to sales in the whole system.

Minimising delivery costs of assortments. Since a wholesaler carries massed stocks from many manufacturers, he can, by adjusting the range and the conditions of sale, deliver at a lower per unti cost than any manufacturer. This function may also be performed by a specialist warehousing and transport firm.

Minimising transaction costs. The principle of minimising contacts also applies to billing and collection costs. Since order sizes between manufacturer and wholesaler are increased, the number of manufacturer transactions is minimised, as is the number of transactions of retailers.[37]

Not all wholesalers perform the same functions or groups of functions as is evident from the diagram of the channels of distribution of the West German grain supply in Figure 6.1. A taxonomy of the wholesaling trade faces obstacles of inclusion and exclusion, for some of the wholesale functions can be performed by manufacturers or retailer, or by specialists in one of the functions such as transport, warehousing or selling. In

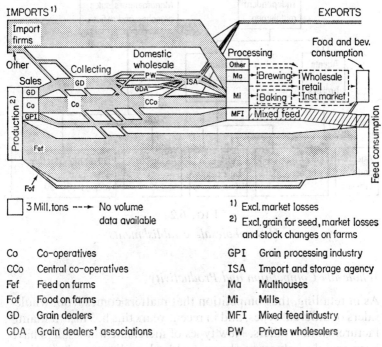

Co	Co-operatives		GPI	Grain processing industry
CCo	Central co-operatives		ISA	Import and storage agency
Fef	Feed on farms		Ma	Malthouses
Fof	Food on farms		Mi	Mills
GD	Grain dealers		MFI	Mixed feed industry
GDA	Grain dealers' associations		PW	Private wholesalers

FIG. 6.1 *Marketing channels for grain, West Germany, 1967–8*

addition, manufacturers may perform some of the wholesale functions of other manufacturers under a contractual arrangement such as factoring, and retailers may similarly serve as wholesalers to other retailers.

The Census of Wholesale Distribution (1950, 1965) simply distinguishes wholesale firms by size, product group, and according to whether they carry stocks. Other systems also distinguish them by type of ownership or function.

The U.S. Bureau of Census used a classification outlined by Bucklin,[38] and shown in Figure 6.2.

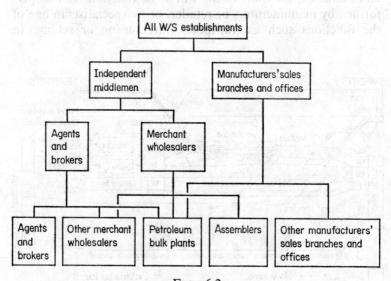

FIG. 6.2
U.S. wholesale establishments

Wholesale Competition and Productivity

As in retailing, the competition that matters comes from wholesalers of different types, and in recent years this has meant manufacturers and retailers. New types of merchant wholesalers have been mainly voluntary chains and cash-and-carry wholesalers, who have tended to specialise in the smaller outlets, or in supplying the catering trade. In times of economic downturn, transients and newcomers are attracted to deal with the jobbing of manufacturers' stock which must be sold quickly. Some remain in the trade once the recession has passed, developing their own innovation which allows them to compete on price. The general effect of non-merchant-wholesaler competition has been to reduce the volume of trade available to merchant wholesalers in urban areas, and compel them to operate in suburban and rural areas, as Bucklin demonstrates for the United States.[39]

Concentration

Traditional measures of concentration cannot be used on the
U.K. Census data, but an alternative method making use of the
log-normal (Pareto) curve, by which 80 per cent of the sales will
normally be made by 20 per cent of the business units, permits
some observation to be made. The data from the census have
been presented in Table 6.2.

TABLE 6.2 *Distribution of wholesale trade*

Kind of business	Volume of sales (per cent)		Proportion of business units (per cent)
Grocery	81·9	made by	13·8
Beer, wine and spirits	83·2	,,	22·4
Meat	85·3	,,	27·2
Clothing and textiles	74·5	,,	18·5
Hardware and electrical	75·5	,,	21·9
Petroleum	97·7	,,	16·5
Coal merchants	87·6	,,	16·3
Corn, seed and agricultural merchants	46·0	,,	17·5
Ores and metals	85·0	,,	17·1
Timber	86·9	,,	31·8
Industrial machinery	80·2	,,	18·6
Other industrial materials	88·6	,,	15·4

SOURCE: 'Inquiry into the Wholesale Trades 1965' (adapted), *Board
of Trade Journal* (26 July 1968).

Barriers to Entry

Conditions vary from one product group to another – as in
retailing. In some cases exclusive dealing arrangements of highly
concentrated manufacturing industry can make it difficult to
enter the market, as in magazine publishing, motor-car dealer-
ships, bicycles, and many other industrial products. In some
cases the barrier may be surmounted by importing supplies from
other Common Market countries under the protection of E.E.C.
laws on competition, or from associated members of the E.E.C.

Wholesale Policies

Wholesalers have to solve very similar problems concerning attractiveness and deterrence, with differences appearing only in the list of factors in each function. Since wholesaling requires considerable warehouse space, and proximity to the market centre, there are relatively few locations in any one centre. This results in agglomerations of similar-type wholesalers in fairly well defined wholesaling sectors of the city, and with increases in the population served, wholesalers become more specialised in product line, in size of order handled, or in the functions performed. As the volume of business available diminishes, they seek to take over more functions previously performed by manufacturer or retailer, expand their assortment, or seek cost savings through co-operation either horizontally or vertically.[40]

VERTICAL MARKETING SYSTEMS

In the distribution of products like foodstuffs and beverages, the channels which convey the commodities to the food processor may be as important as those which convey the packaged product to the consumer. The processing function may move between members of the channel, just as the stockholding function may move, affecting costs, productivity or structure of the channel. The national government takes a close interest in channels such as these where the price of basic staples is likely to be affected by firms' policies and practices. Firms who have integrated, or seek to integrate vertically, also have an interest in what happens upstream as well as downstream in their channels.

In studying the whole marketing system for a commodity, the first problem, identified by Jeffreys,[41] is to define the product so as to determine the starting point of the channel, since some can be quite lengthy. One project which examined the marketing of housebuilding materials in the United States[42] involved tracing the materials backward from the building site to the source, in order to eliminate the problem of distinguishing types of customers and products which would not be used in housebuilding. This resulted in flow charts, one for each of forty-three materials, with a product monograph to supplement the data on the chart. Since that time many others have been completed, such as the study of fish distribution in Tanzania.[43]

As a result of such studies, the need emerged for a method of classifying those flows through different channels, a method more specific than the three main channels adopted by Jeffreys, namely 'direct to consumer', 'direct to retailer', and 'sales through wholesalers'. Such generalisations fail to capture the detail of how the functions are shared between the different types of intermediaries. The functions which are completed in any transaction were listed by Bucklin as follows[44]

The transfer of merchandise (the physical goods);
The transfer of title;
Negotiations (the transfer of orders);
The transfer of information; and
The transfer of funds.

Since they are performed by a succession of business entities,

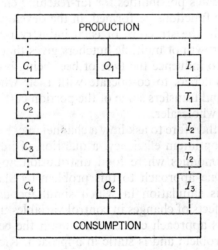

Functional act symbols

C Communication
O Ownership
T Transit
I Inventory

Flow symbols

—·—·— Exchange rights
——— Title
------ Physical product

FIG. 6.3 *Functional structure flow chart*

they have also been referred to as flows by other writers. Commodity channels now require five separate descriptions of the flows of each functional element of the channel, and therefore some kind of notation system to handle this.

One notation method suggested by Gill[45] was to use 'graph theory', thus making the network of each flow meanable to mathematical methods for the purpose of identifying existing inefficiencies. Another suggested by Bucklin[46] used algebraic notation to develop a taxonomy suitable for comparing channel structures of different commodities, or of the same commodity over a period of time. None of these methods suggested have proved attractive enough to generate analytical studies of commodity channels. Until now, comparisons have been limited to descriptions of flows as a means of identifying the costs involved with a view to minimising these, or to inter-nation comparisons to provide insights for a marketing strategy in a new market.[47]

The large number of entities involved in such vertical marketing systems creates possibilities for far-reaching changes in the location of the functions performed, in the development of the product, and in the structure of each industry involved. For example, the growth of multiple butchers gives that retail institution power to influence the type of beef being bred, requires independent butchers to co-operate with their wholesalers to reduce costs, and transfers some of the portion cutting from the retailer to the wholesaler.

It is natural therefore to ask how a channel may be so ordered as to achieve optimum efficiency, a question of importance in developing economies where food distribution appears to be inefficient.[48] One approach to this problem by Slater[49] was a general-systems simulation in which simultaneous equations describe the effects of changes in control variables upon market processes. This approach concentrates upon the economic aspects of the problem and is static in approach. Richartz[50] suggested, in a path-finding paper, that game theory might be used to determine what would happen competitively when changes are introduced by one firm at one level in the channel, thus opening up a route to combining economic and social systems.

FUNCTIONS OF CHANNELS

To view a set of business entities operating at different levels in the channel of distribution as being performers of functions might seem offensive to entrepreneurs devising different and attractive offers. Nevertheless, that the entities do perform functions, and do add utility as a result of doing so, is the main justification for their existence. What the functions are has also been much debated and the literature contains a large number of different lists of the functions, or of the kinds of inputs associated with effecting change.[51] It is fairly easy to agree on the more obvious functions such as transportation, stockholding and communications. Disagreement comes when considering price which it can be argued is a function of variables such as supply and demand, or the value produced by the operation of all the exchange functions, namely the work involved in effecting an exchange.

For the purpose of this section a function is viewed as the work which is done towards effecting the exchange of a product whose form is not to be changed any further. This allows processing to be ignored, and produces the following list:

Physical movement of goods, including temporary storage;
Stockholding, where the function is to postpone consumption or to speculate against future consumption;
Sorting, including breaking bulk;
Communication and contact; and
Order and payment processes by both buyer and seller.

All of these functions can be seen to have cost inputs and measurable outputs, though this quality may be somewhat tenuous in the case of communication. Such a statement of functions, while eliminating the creative elements of an attractive selling offer with a consequent effect on price, does make possible a cost-minimising approach to distribution channels such as was attempted on a theoretical model by Baligh and Richartz.[52]

Physical Distribution

Each of the functions has been subject to input–output type studies with a view to determining the most efficient method, but none more than the function of physical distribution, involving transport, storage and stockholding. In this function, the main problem areas are:

(1) Design of the facilities to be used for a given throughput;
(2) Establishment of parameters for decisions; and
(3) Issue and operation of orders based on these parame.ers.

The field of study is basically 'operations research' and is well documented.[53] Computer companies, whose equipment is ideally suited to dealing with the computations involved, have designed systems for large companies which will accept the data on orders received, and transform it into delivery schedules, invoices and production orders, while up-dating stock lists, purchase requirements, production schedules and so on.

The technology involved may soon reach its maximum in achieving economies of scale, as was suggested by Heskitt,[54] and emphasis will be shifted to achieving economies within channels by means of closer integration.

For the smaller firm, the problems are not associated with owning facilities, but rather with choosing specialists who will handle the physical distribution on a contract. This introduces the need for developing criteria as to the purchase of these services and to studies of these criteria.[55]

Stockholding. Where speculation is involved in stockholding, the principles involved have already been set out by Bucklin, but the efficient operation of this function involves an element of prediction as to the behaviour of demand and supply in respect of price if a stockholding policy is to be evolved. Once this has been done, the function becomes a straightforward warehousing function, in which warehousing costs are minimised for a given throughput.[56]

Sorting. Sorting and assorting are functions carried out mainly by wholesalers and retailers, but also to some extent by manufacturers who perform some wholesale functions. The problem of optimising the assortment at the level of the firm was dealt with as shelf-space allocation, and the same approach may be used to optimise the sorting function in any setting.

Communication and Contact. The wholesaler's contribution to minimising information costs has already been noted, but where a firm chooses to disseminate information without wholesalers, they must be interested in making studies of the cost of doing so.[57] The activities of salesmen in this function are open to operations-research techniques to minimise non-selling activities and costs using journey planning, and maximising the outputs of selling activities by regulating the length and frequency of call, or by specialising the selling activities. Studies of these activities together with studies of advertising effectiveness may be dealt with exhaustively elsewhere in the text.

Orders and payment processes. These two functions are linked together, since they tend to be performed by administrators working closely together within the buying and the selling entities. There is a fairly well established relationship between the flow of orders and cash which becomes important in the firm's strategy, and between average order size and the administrative costs of buying and selling. The size of the order-filling capability of a firm was modelled by Baligh and Richartz[58] showing the link between the statistical distribution of orders and inventories. Empirical work in this area has been mostly at the level of the firm, using the skills of methods engineers and cost accountants to reduce the system delays and the administrative costs. Marketing managers have been quick to appreciate the benefits of improving their service level to customers using better order-processing methods.

Trends in Efficiency

'Operations research', an important tool for modelling input and output behaviour, tends to isolate a problem, drawing boundaries with other related functions. The consequence has been that problems solved in one functional area produced new problems in others. To enlarge the boundaries of the problem creates an immense computation which can only be justified by immense savings, so that the large company working closely with the computer company is the most likely to persist in this path. One of the consequences of the recognition of the problem has been the development of a total concept for the distribution function in which all of the functions mentioned are considered together.

Accounting methods of cost analysis, particularly of functional cost analysis, where a function output can be identified, is much more attractive to the smaller firm. The method is within the competence of most accountants, using well-tried costing techniques whose benefits and failings are known.[59] Computer companies now adapt their physical-distribution routines to include cost analysis in their data print-out, or to signal the variances from a norm established by budget or work study.

SOCIAL AND POLITICAL SYSTEM

The idea of exchange having a socio-political basis was suggested by Polyani,[60] an anthropologist who saw that man's economy was submerged in his social relationships, man acting so as to safeguard his social standing, his social claims, his social assets and valuing material goods in so far as they serve this end. When a group of retailers act together to preserve their social assets, as did the *Poujadists* of France, they then become part of a political system, aiming to preserve the social as well as the economic elements of their life.

Components of the System

Boddewyn[61] devised a framework for this type of study in management, a framework capable of being adapted, as he says, to any societal institution. He suggested that the social system involves concepts as follows:

(a) *Actors* – the participants in the social or political system;
(b) *Processes* – what the participants do;
(c) *Structures* – how they relate to one another;
(d) *Functions* – the contribution made by the participants; and
(e) *Interaction with the environment* – within which they must react.

(a) *Actors.* Classification systems for the actors have only a rudimentary development using economic criteria as in the Census, or the degree of participation in the system as in Kriesberg's study of steel distributors when he coined the expressions 'insiders', 'strivers', 'complementors' and 'transients'.[62]

The problem is to avoid economic generalisations associated with terms like 'small retailer' without being caught in the trap of specification.

Since the actors are essentially organisations rather than individuals, three levels of aggregation are possible. The first is that of the firm, the second is the group of firms which make up a system, and the third a larger aggregation such as an industry. The second level, that of the organisational cluster, is most commonly used as a concept in examining the processes.[63]

(b) *Processes*. The study of behaviour in a social system by the actors of the system is properly the province of the social scientist. The study of social behaviour in a distribution system, consisting as it does of independent organisations with different sets of roles,[64] has formed only a small part of that field of study.[65] The need for such studies is apparent from the attempts of members of distribution channels to solve their inter-organisational conflicts by means of vertical integration, a solution which often throws up new intra-organisational problems.

Behavioural research covers the following sub-sets: (1) the pattern of forming behaviour and the forces which are active in the process; (2) descriptions of aggregate behaviour patterns, and the distribution of patterns of behaviour so described; and (3) the relationship between one aggregate of behaviour patterns and other aggregates.[66]

Evan[67] developed the idea of behaviour patterns which had become established as roles, applying it to the organisations with which a channel member interacts to constitute the organisation-set. The behaviour of channel members is determined by the pre-scriptions of members of its organisation-set, by their sanctions for conforming and non-conforming behaviour, and by the channel member's conception of what his own behaviour should be.

(c) *Structures*. The relationship between channel members pro-voked a considerable volume of hypotheses in the 1970s, much of it stemming from work by Palamountain in 1955.[68] These relationships are of interdependency, where one member's social gains may be another member's social losses. At any time the system will exhibit evidence of co-operation between members, while at other times conflict will appear to threaten the system's very existence. Both conflict as a stimulus to creativity and re-alignment, and co-operation as a cost-saving, routinising, force are necessary processes in the system.

Conflict originates in deviations from established behaviour patterns, changed expectations of channel members, changed perceptions of others' behaviour, extensions of the domain of one member, or ineffective communication.[69]

Co-operation follows when the organisations come to terms with the goals of the total system, and with the goals of the most powerful member in the system. Various methods may be used by the most powerful member to bring about this situation, or where there is no one single powerful member, as often happens among wholesalers or retailers, the result will be a formalised structure for co-operation.

The processes of conflict and co-operation exhibit the presence of power and dependence. Various bases of power have been, identified – expected rewards and costs, coercion, expertness legitimacy and identification – and are reviewed by Wilkinson.[70] For a considerable period, it was assumed that the most powerful channel member was the manufacturer[71] by virtue of his being the original title holder to goods desired by the consumer, but with the increase in the purchase power of retail buyers, the most powerful member of some vertical channel systems is now the multiple retailer. This has produced a revision of theory as to the dynamics of power[72] in which the interdependency of members is re-emphasised.

(d) *Functions.* One purpose of co-operation is to effect the ex-change between producer and consumer at a lower cost than a direct exchange. This economic function has already been explored. The system, however, has a social function. Wittreich,[73] commenting on the distributor's attitude to money, power and status, noted a satisficing approach, a self-imposed limit on the extent of their gains being common among them. Galbraith and Holton[74] commented on the 'live and let live' attitude of Puerto Rican retailers, who regarded themselves as advisers and confi-dants to their customers, being community leaders in many ways. The social goals of large retailers such as Marks and Spencer have also been revealed in biographies of the organisations, but to date little research other than descriptive narratives have been produced to identify the contribution made by the channels of distribution to the social assets of the participants, and those whom they serve.

(c) *Interaction with the environment*. Comparative studies in distribution have demonstrated that distribution institutions are a reflection of the particular environment in which they are found.[75] The national culture is imprinted on the customs and traditions of trade between members of a distribution channel to the point where sellers from one country, attempting to make themselves acceptable to buyers in another, have to spend some time adapting their behaviour to the social system of the buyers. Among Asian traders in East Africa, or Chinese traders in Indonesia, there exists a brotherhood, a trusting relationship born of their being strangers in a strange land. Seldom fully integrated with the social system of their adopted country, they are hated and distrusted by the local population, yet they continue to perform their economic function efficiently.[76] Studies of these distributive systems have helped to identify the social and political nature of the distribution in the United Kingdom.

Communications

In any system, the accurate, timely and dependable flow of information is a necessary aspect of the organisation's survival. The problems which arise in a distribution communications network are similar to those of other systems, and have been listed as follows:[77]

Overload. When the limit of capacity is reached, additional information may be ignored or misunderstood. The problem of detailing an ever-increasing range of new drugs to an overworked doctor exemplifies this.

Secrecy. Competitive advantage requires some members of channels to be excluded from information while others are included. Since the communication network is 'open' it may force the creation of a separate sub-system.

Timing. Information may be premature, or aged, and be of less value to the user with a resulting loss of communication effectiveness.

Perceptual differences. Different types of channel members take different views of each others' information. The urgency of the retailer may be discounted by the manufacturer, while direction for storage and display may be regarded as an interference with the retailer's expertise.

MACROECONOMICS OF DISTRIBUTION CHANNELS

Any examination of a system composed of separate business entities raises the question of improving the system by some degree of integration stimulated by government. Some believe that only completely planned economies, or completely market (unplanned) economies, can work. Others believe that governments have a role in regulating the operation of key industries within an otherwise market economy.

In a planned economy, the production and consumption of the economic system are determined by a central planning office. Supply and demand are balanced by controlling the wages and prices in the system without any reference to the creation of surpluses in any one unit, or at any one level.[78] The concept of surplus in one entity is unnecessary since, like a vertically integrated market system, the whole system is responsible for producing the surplus which is to be invested in the future.[79]

The marketing part of such a system usually has a minor role – this is for two reasons. First there is no competition with alternative suppliers, and second the consumers' intakes have been predetermined to a considerable extent by the production plan. The distributors still require to fulfil the functions performed in market economies, but with more constraints operating on their freedom to select and negotiate with their suppliers in creating assortments, in the same way that the wholly owned vertical market system of a food supplier in a market economy operates.

A completely unplanned economy is not so common, although Jeffreys[80] found that respondents in his 1949 enquiry regarded 1938 as the pinnacle of a free economy. Since that time, governments have intervened in the free market to regulate the prices, quality and quantity of goods sold, the places and circumstances under which they may be sold, the profit which may be made and the portion of the business which may be inherited.

Other regulations govern competition between business entities with a view to reducing the power of monopolies in their price and profit decisions. This covers the making of agreements in restraint of trade, the merging of competing firms and the taking into public ownership of key industries in the economy.

Protection of the consumer is also achieved by regulating product descriptions, or claims for products, the additives in food products and the composition of pharmaceutical products, to mention but a few.

Protection for those employed in channels of distribution covers wages, holidays, hours of work, the working environment and its facilities, and conditions of dismissal, in laws which are specific in some cases to retail distribution, transport and warehousing.

With that volume of regulation, the distribution system nevertheless continues to attract new entrants, to evolve, to adapt itself to changing market and economic conditions and to cope with the demands made on it by producers and consumers alike. It copes with shortages of supply caused by crop failures or disaster, or the planning failures of planned economies, and appears, in spite of being labour intensive, to continue to improve its productivity.

Development of Channels

Over a very long period, centuries rather than decades, students have noticed a regular pattern of channel development. In primitive economies with few specialisms, the channel is short and direct, farmers supplying produce directly to consumers in an open market-place. With an increasing separation of farming and consumption, the retailer takes over the marketing function, and also some of the processing of the consumer. At the next stage in economic growth, the processing and retailing are separated and a distinct channel can be identified:

Farmer → Processor → Retailer → Consumer.

Further lengthening of the channel by the insertion of wholesalers is also accompanied by town growth, which increases the average distance of all farmers from the processor, and the processor from the retailer, until no further economies may be obtained. Now the channel members look for economies through increased scale brought about by technology or by co-operation. The scale increases now permit a shortening of channels as the larger firms take back these functions previously performed by a specialist, usually the wholesaler.

Channel Life Cycle

These developments apply mainly to commodity channels which can be identified closely with food and beverages. The same kind of process can also be detected in the development of the firm's distribution channels as output increases in volume and variety, beginning with a single product produced on a small scale (see Figure 6.4). When first set up, the firm's channels tend to be short, distribution taking place mainly in the market nearest the factory. With growth of sales, goods are delivered further afield using specialist transport firms. Further growth requires the assistance of wholesalers or selling agents, while a further stage of growth sees the firm's sales force extended and dependence on intermediaries reduced. Finally the firm acquires a vertically integrated distribution network.

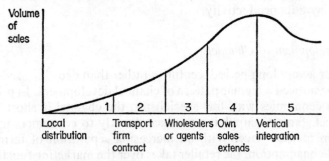

FIG. 6.4 *Distribution-channel life cycle*

Innovations in Channels

Innovations by new entrants to channels have been noted,[81] but some innovations can also be attributed to channel incumbents, for efficient channel management will always seek to minimise costs and maximise sales. Some innovations which have been noted are:

Delivering other companies' complementary products to the same outlets;

Combining sales forces with a complementary firm;

Sub-contracting space capacity in physical distribution

Providing services to intermediaries (merchandising, accounting);

Factoring accounts for other companies;

Factoring products for other companies; and

Voluntary integration of data systems.

Academic interest in innovation is extended to the sources, spread, and reaction to it.[82]

THE FIRM AND ITS DISTRIBUTION CHANNEL

The distribution-channel decisions of the firm may be separated into 'channel design' and 'channel management', with each decision interacting with the other.

Channel Design

The designs of channels of distribution to be used by the firm is an integral part of the total marketing strategy, just as the marketing strategy is an integral part of the firm's business policy. The initial design of channels may have been subordinate to other aspects of policy, but once established the channels assume a major role in shaping the other aspects of the marketing mix. Design changes occur at infrequent intervals, as indicated in the channel life cycle, and are accompanied by other major changes in the marketing mix.

The design and subsequent redesign of distribution channels, involving as it does elements within the company as well as part of all of organisations outside the company, may cover any or all of the five flows which together constitute the exchange transactions. The need for redesign may arise out of:

(a) Failure of one member of the channel to satisfy the expectations of other members;

(b) An increase in the level of expectations of one channel member as a result of (i) offers of increased expectations by competitors, and (ii) changes in the perceptions of any of the channel members.

In some cases, the redesign may be avoided by renegotiating with the channel member involved so that a new basis for co-operation is established.

Channels may be designed following the flow concept[83] discussed under vertical marketing systems, whereby decisions are made concerning each of the five flows of goods, title, orders information and funds.

The variables affecting the design are:

(A) *Endogenous variables*

    (1) Availability of product ideas (patents, designs, licences, contracts);
    (2) Physical resources and flexibility of allocation;
    (3) Personnel skills and their flexibility; and
    (4) Stakeholder expectations.

(B) *Exogenous variables*

    (1) Competing products and rate of innovation;
    (2) Physical resources of competitors;
    (3) Personnel skills of competitors;
    (4) The intermediaries, their size, numbers, resources and perceptions; and
    (5) The end users, their purchase behaviour, numbers, growth rate.

Variables 1, 2 and 3 in the second list provide a range against which the corresponding variables of the firm may be fitted to give a rating of the power of the firm in the channel. The relationship of the variables to each other is then expressed in Figure 6.5.

It can be seen from this model that most distribution decisions can be taken on the basis of a knowledge of intermediaries available and of stakeholder expectations, while ignoring the possibility of increasing the number of intermediaries immediately available through skilful manipulation of resources allocated to the important variables listed 1, 2 and 3.

In coming to a decision on design, one method, outlined by Berg,[84] advocates a five-step procedure:

    (1) Factor the strategic situation in which the key factors involved in channel strategy are isolated;

(2) Convert the key factors into activity requirements, or functions which must be performed;

(3) Group the functions into work units suitable for the intermediaries;

(4) Allocate the functions to intermediaries who are available and open to negotiation; and

(5) Designate the appropriate structural relationship by identifying the activities which need to be controlled in the intermediaries.

In the case of a redesign, there is a prior need to chart the existing channel systems so that the system may be thoroughly understood, the functions performed by each intermediary clearly defined, and system duplication or redundancy noted.

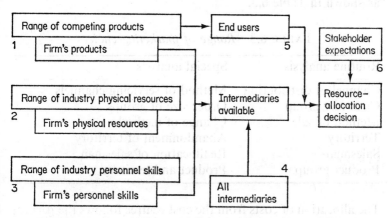

FIG. 6.5   *Cause–effect model of variables in channel design*

Channel Management

Implicit in the idea of channel management is the twofold process of cost minimisation and sales maximisation, objectives which may be incompatible, but which are capable of optimisation at that point where marginal revenue equals marginal cost. A first requirement, therefore, is information on the costs and profits involved in distribution, for without information on costs, any attempts to evaluate the effectiveness of selected channels must be open to doubt, and the control of efficiency made suspect.

The methodology of cost accounting is well documented[85] with its adaptation to distribution being fairly simple.[86] The technique consists of establishing, first, cost centres of activities to which all the cost of that activity may be allocated. Typically this would consist of transport, personal selling, sales administration, warehousing, and credit and collection.

This set of cost centres in itself will provide information useful in the control of each of these activities, since the actual cost per unit of output may be calculated and controlled through a budget system. This represents no more than the normal costing and budgeting practices.

Distribution cost analysis requires new classifications to be set up, classifications based the channels being used, but they may be extended to cover the whole range of marketing choices as shown in Table 6.3.

TABLE 6.3 *Range of marketing choices*

Routine analysis	Special analysis
Channel of distribution	Method of servicing channels
Customer group	Order size of groups
Method of sale	Change of method
Territory	Abandonment of territory
Salesman	Reallocation of salesman
Product group	Product and territory

The allocation of costs from the cost centres follows the general principles of cost allocation used in costing for direct and indirect costs. In certain cases like advertising, where there is no clear relationship between the cost centre and the channel used, the cost may be left unallocated and treated as an overhead requiring a contribution from profit-making activities. A typical cost analysis is provided in Table 6.4.

Sales analysis. In the example used, it is a simple matter to discover the value of sales to these different types of customers, but as further demands are made for sales analysis – methods of sale, type of sales representatives, territory and product – computer assistance may be required.

Computer involvement imposes certain requirements on data

capture so that they may be easily processed, the most common condition being that data are captured at the moment they are first raised as a customer's order within the firm. For the firm with a computer, this problem will already have been foreseen by the computer supplier if the computer was being used in connection with production and inventory control.

TABLE 6.4   *Retail customer group – cost analysis*

Function Retail sales value	Small indepen-dents £45,000	Large indepen-dents £145,000	Mul-tiples £500,000	Co-ops £60,000	Total £750,000
Personal selling costs	3000	8000	24000	5000	40000
Sales administration:					
Supervision	450	1200	3600	750	6000
Order processing	600	1000	1000	400	3000
Credit and collection	1100	1700	3700	1000	7500
Advertising and promotion					
Consumer media	3600	11600	40000	4800	600
Trade media	120	400	1320	160	2000
Point of Sale	600	1000	3000	400	5000
Sales deductions					
Retail margins and discounts	8100	29000	125000	13200	175300
Physical distribution					
Stockholding costs	2250	7250	25000	3000	37500
Transport	1500	2500	10500	1500	16000
Cost of production (43·03% SP)	19364	62393	215125	25818	322700
Total costs	40684	126043	452245	56128	675000
Net profit contribution	4316	18957	47755	3972	75000
Percentage of retail sales	9·59	13·07	9·55	6·62	10

For companies where computer assistance cannot be justified, the data may still be captured at the moment of order with an order form capable of being converted easily to machine-usable data, taking the advice of a machine supplier or a computer bureau.

Evaluation of effectiveness. Cost analysis can lead to cost-minimisation procedures for each cost centre, but it cannot except through long-term-trend analysis produce ideas for re-allocation of resources to cost centres such as switching from a transport–warehouse system to a transport-only system. It cannot prove that reducing call frequencies to small retailers will result in increased profits because the effect of minimising costs on sales is generally unknown. Some optimising procedures have used sales-trend analysis[87] at the level of the firm, while others have used assumptions to build a computer model.[88]

In the short term, cost analysis will provide data for any experiments in resource allocation so that the 'before and after' situation can be clearly seen. There is no way to exclude creativity from the design of channels except perhaps by expensive and complex model-building, where there is a theoretical prospect of 'running the model' for experimental purposes. Models, however, are notorious for being unable to cope with dynamic situations involving organisations outside of the firm.

SUMMARY

In this chapter, the retailing and wholesaling industries have been depicted as a group of highly competitive entrepreneurs, actively seeking to improve their efficiency and their service. New interest in the retail function at the level of the firm has encouraged researchers to use the tools of economics and mathematics to improve operational efficiency. The presence of the wholesaler is justified, but research in operational efficiency at the level of the firm is needed.

The study of channels which includes processors promises to yield new insights into the location of all the functions performed, but the increasing complexity of long channels calls for new tools to be developed. The functions performed in the systems have generally been well researched since they present engineering-type problems involving inputs and outputs amenable to mathematical analysis.

The societal aspects of channels, a new area of study still in the hands of the social scientists, presents old problems in a different light for all involved in channels, but particularly for the channel leaders, whose actions affect every member.

The place of channels in the nation's economy, their development and the purpose of government intervention was considered while the design and management of the firm's channels was explored briefly

Chapter 7
Diffusion Theory and Marketing

INTRODUCTION

A natural consequence of the marketing concept, with its emphasis upon the determination of consumer wants and the deployment of resources to match these wants, is that the marketing function places particular stress upon new-product development. In this chapter we will attempt to demonstrate that the problems associated with introducing new products into the market-place appear to be remarkably similar to those experienced in gaining acceptance for innovations in other areas of activity. This being so, one might reasonably anticipate that there are considerable benefits to be gained by studying the process by which other innovations appear to secure acceptance as a basis for enhancing consumer reaction to new products.

The process by which innovations spread through a population of users or adopters is generally termed 'diffusion'. Accordingly, in this chapter we first consider the evolution of the diffusion research tradition as a preliminary to examining the marketing variant which is normally referred to as the 'product-life-cycle concept'. In turn, this examination leads us to enquire whether it is possible to operationalise the product-life-cycle concept and thereby make it a useful tool for marketing managers concerned with new-product development. To this end we describe briefly our own model of the adoption process which attempts to synthesise both economic and behavioural variables and so suggests how marketing may usefully borrow from other disciplines in developing valid theory of its own.

THE EVOLUTION OF THE DIFFUSION RESEARCH TRADITION[1]

The earliest research into the process of diffusion appears to have been triggered off by the interest of anthropologists in the spread of ideas between societies. This interest, which began to gather momentum at the beginning of this century, set out to determine whether particular ideas, activities and patterns of behaviour were transferred from society to society or were the result of parallel thought development. Essentially, the thrust of this work was historical and descriptive and laid greater emphasis upon the social consequences of the innovation. None the less certain important generalisations were advanced including one which has formed the foundation for much subsequent research, namely that acceptance of an innovation depends very much upon the prospective adopter's culture. Thus closed or traditional systems were found to hinder diffusion whilst open or modern social systems appear to stimulate it.

One of the earliest contributors to social theories of diffusion was Gabriel Tarde, whose *Laws of Imitations* was published in 1903.[2] In this work Tarde makes several novel proposals which have been very influential in shaping the development of diffusion theory, including the proposition that if adoptions of an innovation are plotted against time from introduction to complete diffusion they will assume the characteristics of a normal distribution, or if plotted cumulatively assume the familiar S-shaped curve which characterises the product life cycle. Tarde is also to be credited with identifying the relationship between cosmopoliteness and early adoption and of formulating the concept of the 'opinion leader' as a member of a social system to whom others look for advice.

During the 1920s a large number of studies were undertaken by empirically minded sociologists most of which were concerned with the tracing of a specific innovation through a population of adopters. With the benefit of hindsight one of the surprising features of this period of development of diffusion theory is that there was very little, if any, transfer of ideas from one branch of research to another. Thus only recently has any attempt been made to integrate the various findings into a single theory of diffusion.[3]

One of the major foundations of this newly emergent integrated theory are the findings of the rural sociologists. By the early 1960s contributions from this area numbered several hundred, many of which replicate the classic study of Ryan and Gross.[4] Among the many contributions of this study three have had a lasting impact:

(1) The concept of adopter classification into categories;

(2) The determination of the social characteristics which identified the earliest and latest adopters; and

(3) Recognition and statement of the deliberate nature of the decision to adopt an innovation.

A second major source of contributions to diffusion theory was provided by the area of medical sociology. Perhaps the most famous study in this area was that undertaken by Coleman, Katz and Menzel which is often identified as the Columbia University Drug Study or the 'Gammamyn' Study.[5] Perhaps the most significant contribution from this study was the establishment of a positive relationship between opinion leadership and innovativeness.

A survey of contributions from other areas such as that undertaken by Rogers[6] would seem to suggest that they have made very little original contribution to major concepts developed in rural and medical sociology. Thus, whilst educationists have been responsible for a very large numbers of studies, these tend to have built upon, and confirmed, the findings of other researchers. Similarly in the marketing area the main thrust has been in the application of extant concepts in an attempt to reduce the high failure rate associated with the introduction of new products. More recently, however, there have been indications that this research is making an original contribution of its own in the field of what might be termed the 'characteristics of innovation area'.

As mentioned earlier Everett Rogers made an invaluable contribution to diffusion research by summarising and pulling together contributions of the various and diverse research traditions. Certainly it is to Rogers that we owe a major debt for singling out the definitions and major concepts which now enjoy such wide currency amongst marketers. Particularly worthy of mention are his definition of diffusion, the stages in the adoption process, the five dimensions of an innovation and development of the concept of 'adoptive categories' in pursuit of an attempt to define an innovator profile. We review briefly these concepts below.

THE DIFFUSION PROCESS

The characteristics of the diffusion process may be summed up as: (1) acceptance (2) over time (3) of some specific item (4) by adopting units – individuals or groups – (5) linked to communication channels (6) to a social structure (7) to a given system of values. In this context acceptance is probably best defined as 'continued use'. Thus, while purchase of a durable good would count as acceptance or adoption, first purchase of a low-price consumable item might only amount to a trial such that adoption would only be assumed given repeated purchase of the item.

Time of adoption is central to the whole concept of diffusion and underlies all attempts to describe the diffusion process in mathematical terms. In the case of most industrial and consumer-durable goods usually it is possible to establish the date of purchase and therefore the elapsed time since first introduction and thereby identify the sequence in which organisations or individuals adopted the item. Unfortunately measurement of elapsed time from first introduction usually depends upon recall in the case of smaller consumable items and is a much less reliable guide to the sequence in which individuals actually adopted an innovation than is the case with industrial goods.

The specific item in our definition is the innovation under study while the unit of adoption has traditionally been conceived of as an individual. However, in recent years the role of joint-buying decisions in both the industrial- and household-buying situations has been increasingly recognised and may be expected to play a more important role in future studies. Clearly in the case of joint adoption decisions identification of the roles played by the respective parties to that decision should have a significant effect upon the promotional and selling tactics adopted by an innovator.

The role of channels of communication, social structure and its attendant value system have all been demonstrated to have a major influence upon the diffusion process. It follows, therefore, that in diffusion studies great importance is attached to identifying both the formal and informal channels of communication used by adopters. Similarly, from a marketing viewpoint the social structure defines the boundaries within which items diffuse and so constitute a statement of the total population of potential adopters. Finally, value systems have a major impact on the way in which a given innovation will be viewed by prospective adopters, and the need to achieve consonance between an innovation and a value system in order to achieve adoption is obvious.

STAGES IN THE ADOPTION PROCESS

The assumption underlying the formulation of adoption-process schemes is that consumer acceptance of a product is not an instantaneous or random event, but a distinct mental and behavioural sequence through which the consumer must progress if adoption of a product is to occur

Various representations of the adoption process have been suggested but all have a common aim of dividing up the adoption process into comprehensible parts in order to provide a conceptual framework for the analysis of how and why adopters move from first knowledge of a new idea, to its trial, to a decision as to whether to adopt or reject that idea. In 1955 a committee of rural sociologists defined a sequence of five stages through which an individual passes in coming to an adoption decision, namely; awareness, interest, evaluation, trial and adoption. In a marketing context Lavidge and Steiner[7] propose a six-stage sequence related to three basic psychological states:

Awareness Knowledge	the cognitive dimension
Liking Preference	the affective dimension
Conviction Purchase	the conative dimension

As noted earlier, the purpose of models of the adoption process is to provide an analytical framework, and it is not intended that one should consider the stages as necessarily being equidistant, as the importance attached to each will tend to vary in relation to both product and consumer characteristics. Similarly, while some researchers have suggested that individual stages in the sequence may be omitted in real life, our own preference is to accept the alternative hypothesis that stages cannot be omitted but that the individual adopter may move up several steps simultaneously, thereby collapsing the hierarchy of effects into a shorter time period. This latter explanation enables us to account for deviations such as impulse buying and also for the different weight attached to different stages dependent upon variations in product and consumer characteristics.

A number of other alternative models of the adoption process have been put forward of which perhaps the best known is the marketer's AIDA (Attention, Interest, Desire, Action) model which identifies four stages consisting of attention, interest, desire and action.

The basic adoption-process and hierarchy-of-effects models have been criticised on the grounds that the only certain indication from analysis of many diffusion studies is that awareness always precedes adoption.[8] As a consequence of these criticisms a number of more sophisticated models have been proposed, *inter alia*, by Robertson and Andreasen and Nicosia.[9] Space limitations preclude discussion of these alternative models and the reader should consult the original sources for a discussion of these.[10]

DIMENSIONS OF AN INNOVATION

Another important component of Rogers's model is identification and classification of the five dimensions of an innovation – relative advantage, compatibility, complexity, divisibility and communicability. These dimensions may be defined as follows:

(1) Relative advantage is the degree to which an innovation is superior to the idea it supersedes;

(2) Compatibility is the degree to which innovation is consistent with existing values and past experiences of adopters;

(3) Complexity is the degree to which an innovation is relatively difficult to understand and use;

(4) Divisibility is the degree to which an innovation may be tried on a limited basis; and

(5) Communicability is the degree to which the results of innovation may be diffused to others.

It is important to note that these characteristics must be defined in relative terms depending upon the potential adopter's status, knowledge and perception of the information concerning the innovation which is presented to him. With this proviso it is clear that the greater the relative advantage an innovation possesses, the more compatible it is with a potential adopter's status and beliefs; the less complex it is, the more readily it can be tried without risk to the trialist, and the easier it is to communicate information concerning the nature and affect of an innovation then the more readily it will be understood. At least two observations may be made about this statement. First, the more radical an innovation, the less will be its perceived compatability, divisibility and communicability and the greater its perceived complexity, and therefore the more uncertain its relative advantage; and, second, any predictions concerning the reaction of a given potential adopter will depend very heavily upon our level of knowledge concerning the status of that adopter at the time that he becomes aware of the innovation.

ADOPTER CATEGORIES

Earlier in this chapter it was noted that if one plots the number of adoptions against time from first introduction of an innovation, the resulting distribution is normal. The observed regularity of this distribution led to the use of the parameters of the normal distribution as a basis for classifying adopters into categories. Using standard deviation from the mean, adopters are divided into five groupings as indicated in Figure 7.1, namely innovators, early adopters, early majority, late majority and laggards.

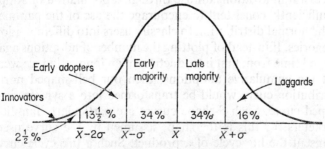

FIG. 7.1 *Adopter categories*

By definition it is tautological that innovators should precede early adopters, that early adopters must precede the majority and so on. In consequence it follows that if we can pre-identify the characteristics of innovators for any given category of innovation, then we may concentrate our marketing efforts upon these individuals. Clearly the potential benefits of such an ability have not been lost upon either the marketing practitioner or his academic colleague. However, while a great deal of empirical work has been undertaken in trying to develop an innovator profile – the results to date of such studies have been both inconclusive and inconsistent – in large measure this inconsistency would seem to stem very largely from a failure to add marketing insights to borrowed concepts. Thus the product, for example, has become almost an adjunct to the researches undertaken rather than being recognised as a key variable *vis-à-vis* the individual consumer characteristics.

Despite some of the deficiencies noted, there can be no doubt that diffusion research has provided a fruitful source of ideas for marketers. Further, having recognised the deficiencies of existing ideas when translated into the marketing context, it becomes possible to see how modification may make such concepts even more useful to the marketing practitioner. In the remainder of this chapter we summarise briefly a modest attempt of our own to make use of diffusion concepts to improve performance when introducing new products into the market-place.

THE PRODUCT LIFE CYCLE

Earlier in this chapter we noted that the manner in which successful innovations diffuse through a population of adopters is sufficiently consistent to encourage the use of the parameters of the normal distribution to classify users into different adopter categories. If instead of plotting the number of adoptions against elapsed time from first introduction of an innovation we were to plot the cumulative adoptions, then our bell-shaped normal-distribution curve would be transformed into a symmetrical S-shaped curve. Such S-shape curves are particularly familiar to marketers for this is the shape assumed by the curve used to represent the life cycle of a product. Such a life cycle curve is reproduced in Figure 7.2 and is traditionally divided into the four phases indicated, namely introduction, growth, maturity and decay.

While most practitioners would readily agree that the product life cycle is an accurate reflection of the manner in which sales of a new product develop, many would question whether the concept has any practical or operational utility. Essentially, such doubts would seem to stem from the observation that in advance one very rarely can predefine the scales appropriate to the plotting of a diffusion curve. Thus if one does not know whether a

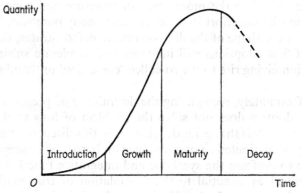

FIG. 7.2   *The product life cycle*

population of adopters will be numbered in tens, hundreds, thousands or tens of thousands, or whether the appropriate unit of time is to be minutes, hours, weeks or even years, one hardly knows how to interpret the early performance of the new product as a basis for predicting the final sales volume and time to complete diffusion. For this reason many practitioners tend to confine the produce-life-cycle concept to the category reserved for many other theoretical constructs which can be labelled as academic, namely 'interesting but irrelevant'.

Our own view, which we develop at some length elsewhere,[11] is that while accepting the possible deficiencies of exponential curves as a forecasting device, the concept does provide one with an enormously useful strategic insight; namely, that the final shape of an exponential function is a direct consequence of its early shape. For example, if one assumes one of the more simple exponential functions, namely a geometric progression, then we would project a doubling of sales for each unit of elapsed time. This being so it follows that if the elapsed time to first purchase from introduction is six months, then we would forecast sales of two more units in the succeeding six-month period, four units in the six months after that, eight units in the following six months, and so on. If, however, the time to first adoption were halved to three months, then sales of fifteen units would be achieved in half the time, that is one year instead of two. Clearly the insight which underlines the search for a consumer innovator profile referred to earlier in this chapter is that the more quickly one pre-identifies potential adopters with a high receptivity to innovation, then the more one can structure and concentrate one's marketing effort in order to secure early purchase. Thereafter, as the shape of the diffusion curve demonstrates, the very fact of first adoptions will influence and accelerate subsequent adoption giving rise to the so-called 'contagion' or 'bandwagon' effect

Unfortunately, recognising the desirability of pre-identifying early adopters does not solve the problem of how to do this. Our own view is that prior deficiencies in this direction may very largely be attributed to over-reliance on borrowed concepts and failure to perform the synthetic and integrative function which we defined as essential to the formulation of true marketing theory in Chapter 2. Specifically, we feel it is essential to pull together economic and behavioural concepts of buying behaviour in order to approximate the real-world situation.

A COMPOSITE MODEL OF BUYER BEHAVIOUR[12]

While recognising the dangers of over-generalisation, the study of the literature of buyer behaviour would seem to warrant division into two distinct categories: a rational/economic model which is strongly associated with the marketing of industrial goods; and a behaviourist model commonly used to describe individual buying behaviour.

Notationally the economic model may be simply represented as:

$$A = f[EC, PC, (I - D)],$$

where A = adoption decision, EC = enabling conditions, PC =

precipitating circumstances, $I =$ economic incentives, $D =$ economic disincentives.

The enabling conditions encompass all those factors which might conceivably be necessary to permit adoption. In both the industrial and the consumer context an obvious precondition is possession of, or access to, sufficient finance to cover purchase or lease of the new product. Other examples of EC in the industrial situation would be relevance to the prospective adopter's current or proposed area of activity, compatibility with the extant production system, and possession of the necessary technical and organisational ability to incorporate the innovation to the firm's operations. In a consumer context, sex, religion, age, physical condition, and so on, may all be highly specific determinants of an innovation's relevance to a potential adopter, and the absence of such an enabling condition would completely preclude any possibility of adoption. Operationally therefore, we may regard EC as the first coarse screen in distinguishing between possible adopters and obvious non-adopters.

Having defined the population of potential adopters, logic dictates that among them some will be in a much more receptive state than others and so will perceive the stimulus (new product) as much stronger than other less receptive prospects. In our model, factors which predispose active consideration of an innovation are identified as precipitating circumstances. Given the existence of the necessary enabling conditions, PC may be thought of as encompassing all these factors which predispose the firm or individual to consider the adoption of an innovation. In terms of the hierarchy-of-effects model of the adoption process, PC coincides with the interest stage as it includes those instants or elements which move the prospective adopter from a possibly passive awareness to an active consideration. In an industrial context the breakdown of plant and equipment, a shortage of fabricated or raw materials, components or sub-assemblies, loss of market share due to price and/or quality differentials, or the opportunity to enter new markets, are but a few of the factors which might precipitate active consideration of an innovation.

Economic incentives and disincentives are specified separately in our model because it is believed that by doing so a better picture of the net economic benefit will emerge than by using a composite variable such as relative advantage. In a purely object-tive world economic logic would seem to demand that if one has a clearly identified need and is presented with a solution which offers a net improvement in one's economic status then one cannot refuse. In reality of course we all know of many instances where such apparently irresistible offers have been flatly rejected for subjective reasons; for example, the works manager who turns down a piece of labour-saving equipment of proven performance on the grounds that attempts to substitute capital equipment for labour would lead to trouble with unions

Because of the role of such subjective factors one might be led to believe that the behaviourist explanation would be more satisfactory than that proposed by the economist. However, as we have already noted earlier in this chapter, a major deficiency of the behaviourist approach to buying decisions is an almost complete neglect of the product characteristics as an influence on the decision. In other words, the behaviourists ignore objective data which clearly are of importance in much the same way as economists neglect the importance of perception. Thus in order to operationalise our economic model of buyer behaviour we need to incorporate in it an additional variable which represents the behavioural response of the potential adopter.

In *Marketing New Industrial Products* we describe at some length a research study undertaken to try and identify the sort of factors which collectively might make up the behavioural response of industrial buying units. While modest success was achieved in terms of defining specific variables which influence the adoption of the two innovations under study, our over-all results clearly indicated a strong probability that these were situation-related. In other words, while our general model of buying behaviour combining both economic and behavioural variables appears to be an acceptable reflection of the real-world situation, it will be incumbent upon individual marketers to define and specify the nature of the sub-variables which comprise the aggregated variable if they are to be able to use the model to assist them with their own new-product marketing programmes. Certainly it seems unlikely that any researcher without direct knowledge and experience of a particular situation in a given market at a given point in time would have the information necessary to operationalise the model.

SUMMARY

As in the other chapters in this part of the book we have attempted to show how concepts and ideas from other disciplines may be used as a basis for thinking about marketing problems. However, our consideration has also indicated that it is unlikely that such ideas will be immediately useful without suitable modification and adaptation.

Part 3
New Directions in Marketing

Chapter 8

Extending the Marketing Concept

INTRODUCTION

To this point we have been concerned with establishing a definition of marketing, with justifying the need for a sound theoretical foundation if the discipline is to grow, and with indicating how marketing has borrowed from other disciplines such as economics and the behavioural sciences in developing such a foundation. In this chapter we examine the extension of marketing thinking beyond the traditional areas with which it is usually associated – the sale of goods and services.

However, before undertaking a review of new areas for the application of the marketing concept, it must be recognised that there are divisions of opinion among practitioners concerned with selling industrial as opposed to consumer goods as to the applicability of a single theory of marketing. Accordingly, we consider the claimed differences between these two branches of marketing and dismiss them as being imaginary rather than real, and more a matter of degree than of principle.

Next, we devote some attention to the marketing of services. While virtually all definitions of marketing explicitly or implicitly subsume services as a category of product, there are differences between the two which merit somewhat fuller consideration than is usually accorded them and which we think are worth spelling out. Certainly there seem to be a number of service industries which have only recently recognised the possible relevance of the marketing concept, banking and insurance for example, while many other professions would still seem to lack any concept of consumer sovereignty and might well benefit from an understanding of marketing principles and practices.

Finally, we turn to consider an even wider spectrum of situations which may be broadly defined as 'non-business' where there would also seem to be scope for putting a marketing approach into use. Thus, while marketing is normally conceived of as a business function in which products or services are made available for purchase by consumers in consideration for a monetary payment, there are many other exchange relationships where the 'seller' is not seeking a monetary reward for his 'product'. The application of marketing ideas borrowed from the business function to non-commercial activities such as health-education programmes, the Church, voluntary organisations and so on, as well as to quasi-commercial situations, are increasingly regarded as a legitimate area for the extension of the marketing concept, and we conclude with a review of some recent contributions to an area which has been termed 'meta marketing'.

INDUSTRIAL VERSUS CONSUMER MARKETING

In Chapter 1 we put forward the view that marketing might be defined as 'a process of exchange between individuals and/or organisations which is concluded to the mutual benefit and satisfaction of the parties' and that such a definition would imply that 'marketing' has existed since the very first exchange relationship was entered into. We also advanced the view that the re-discovery of marketing in the twentieth century is largely due to the physical separation between producer and consumer, which is a direct consequence of mass production and mass consumption, and which has resulted in the evolution of complex and sophisticated institutions and methods to maintain contact between seller and buyer.

This separation is most marked in the case of mass consumption, packaged, convenience goods and it is with these that the 'new' marketing is most closely identified. Thus concepts such as 'market segmentation' and 'test marketing', and techniques such as sales promotion and media advertising, have developed to their present state largely due to the efforts of companies selling soap and detergents, tobacco and confectionery, and convenience foods, be they canned, frozen or freeze dried. It is also companies like Unilever, Proctor & Gamble, Heinz, Nestlé, British-American Tobacco, and the like, which manufacture these types of products, that have been most subject to criticism for the development and use of such marketing techniques – essentially on the grounds that such activities add costs, but not value, and effectively diminish competition in the market-place (that is, marketing costs are seen as a barrier to entry).

Without debating the rights and wrongs of such criticism, it seems to us that many producers of other categories of product wish to dissassociate themselves from possible contamination and so claim that their branch or category of marketing is intrinsically different. Nowhere is this more marked than in the claimed differences between industrial and consumer-goods marketing. Implicitly we reject this contention, for, if it were true, there could be no justification for a book which seeks to prove the need for a sound theoretical basis to the discipline, for, as we indicated in Chapter 2, an essential feature of a theory is that it provides an acceptable general explanation of part of the real world. Explicitly we reject the supposed differences between the two areas on the grounds that premises on which they rest are merely differences in degree, and not in principle.

Thus a common difference between industrial and consumer marketing is claimed to rest in the differing buying motivations which characterise the purchase situation. But, as we endeavoured to show in the last chapter, it is our opinion that all buying decisions are the outcome of a process in which objective data are reviewed in the light of subjective judgement and perception. Because ultimate consumers spend less time evaluating performance criteria as expressed in a technical specification than do industrial buyers this is not to say that they are uncritical of the actual performance and satisfaction achieved. Certainly differences in emphasis upon different facets of the decision process are not sufficient to warrant the assertion that 'rational buying motives dominate the industrial market', which by implication infers that consumer buying is less rational, if not actually irrational. This is an arrogant presumption which destroys much of the force of the anti-marketing school's criticism for it contains the implication that one person is a better judge of another person's satisfaction than is that person himself. Perhaps Oscar Wilde best summarised this arrogance when he commented scathingly that 'An economist is a man that knows the price of everything but the value of nothing.'

A second basis for differentiating between industrial and consumer marketing – that 'industrial products are technically more complex' – has been dealt with in part in the preceding paragraph. Television sets, pocket calculators and quartz watches are all highly complex products purchased with apparent ease by ultimate consumers. Perhaps it is because the latter are using a satisfaction criterion – good reception, rapid computation, accurate time-keeping – that they do not bother unduly with 'how' this is achieved. In an industrial context we rather suspect that the same motives predominate – in fact technical specification is invariably a *sine qua non* for consideration as is an acceptable price range. Having normalised these two criteria it would seem that the industrial buying choice between competing alternatives must rest on other less tangible and more subjective factors such as expected or perceived reliability, quality of after-sales service, and so on.

Very similar arguments may be deployed against claims that there is a greater degree of concentration among industrial buyers (it depends upon the precise nature of the product, for example compare office supplies with the market for locally produced specialty products); that the scale of purchasing is greater (absolutely this is usually true but in relative terms, that is size of purchase *vis-à-vis* disposable assets, the reverse is often true); that industrial buying is a group process (so are many household purchasing decisions); that the role of service is greater (but compare consumer durables like cars, television sets washing machines, etc.); and that credit plays a more important part (again compare consumer-durable purchases).

If we consider some of the concepts and ideas which we are seeking to integrate into a theory of marketing – some of which we have discussed in some detail in preceding chapters – then it would seem that they have equal relevance to both industrial and consumer marketing (and probably to any other branches of marketing as well). The concept of the marketing mix, propounded by Neil Borden,[1] incorporates those areas or elements which all decision-makers must needs consider in developing a strategy irrespective of the nature of their output, namely:

(1) *Product planning*. Policies and procedures relating to
    (a) product lines to be offered – qualities, design, and so on;
    (b) the markets to sell – whom, where, when and in what quantity;

(c) new-product policy – research and development programme.

(2) *Pricing*. Policies and procedures relating to
   (a) the level of prices to adopt;
   (b) the specific prices to adopt (odd–even, etc.);
   (c) price policy – one price or varying price, price main-
       tenance, use of list prices, and so on;
   (d) the margins to adopt – for company or for the trade.

(3) *Branding*. Policies and procedures relating to
   (a) selection of trade marks;
   (b) brand policy – individualised or family brand;
   (c) sale under private brand or unbranded.

(4) *Channels of distribution*. Policies and procedures relating to
   (a) the channels to use between plant and consumer;
   (b) the degree of selectivity among wholesalers and
       retailers;
   (c) efforts to gain co-operation of the trade.

(5) *Personal selling*. Policies and procedures relating to
   (a) the burden to be placed on personal selling and the
       methods to be employed in (i) the manufacturer's
       organization, (ii) the wholesale segment of the trade,
       and (iii) the retail segment of the trade.

(6) *Advertising*. Policies and procedures relating to
   (a) the amount to spend, that is the burden to be placed
       on advertising;
   (b) the copy platform to adopt (i) product image desired,
       and (ii) corporate image desired;
   (c) the mix of advertising – to the trade, through the
       trade, to consumers.

(7) *Promotions*. Policies and procedures relating to
   (a) the burden to place on special selling plans or devices
       directed at or through the trade;
   (b) the form of these devices for consumer promotions,
       for trade promotions.

(8) *Packaging*. Policies and procedures relating to
   (a) formulation of package and label.

(9) *Display*. Policies and procedures relating to
   (a) the burden to be put on display to help effect sales;
   (b) the methods to adopt to secure display.

(10) *Servicing*. Policies and procedures relating to
   (a) providing service needed.

(11) *Physical handling.* Policies and procedures relating to
    (a) warehousing;
    (b) transportation;
    (c) inventories.
(12) *Fact finding and analysis.* Policies and procedures relating to
    (a) the securing, analysis and use of facts in marketing operations.

Similarly, the concept of market segmentation or the general model of buyer behaviour which we propose appears to offer equal benefit to different branches of marketing. In sum, therefore, we feel that it is divisive to pursue differences between consumer and industrial marketing, not because there are no differences but because concentration on dissimilarity can only delay the development of a coherent and integrated theory. Once we have such a theory, then will be the time to increase its sophistication and explanatory power by distinguishing variations or departures from the accepted principles. However, we also feel that when such a time comes it will be found that a crude distinction between industrial and consumer markets will not suffice, for, as the above points suggest, there are likely to be as great if not greater differences within these two categories than there are between them.

THE MARKETING OF SERVICES

As indicated in the introduction to this chapter, most writers on 'marketing' claim that the term 'product' should be regarded as a collective noun which also includes services. In principle, as our dismissal of fundamental differences between industrial and consumer marketing indicates, we accept that any theory of marketing should be capable of application to both products and services. At the same time, it is important to recognise that the development of another splinter group of 'service marketers' has not yet emerged to join the industrial marketers, largely because the transfer of marketing techniques to service industries is of relatively recent origin.

In part this delay may be explained by the more personal nature of many services which has precluded the separation between the main parties to the exchange process – producer and consumer – that brought about the need for new institutions and techniques in the mass-consumption convenience-goods market. Similarly, interest in adopting techniques from the latter fields owes much to a desire to increase the productivity of the service industries.

Just as there are differences in degree in other areas of marketing, so we may anticipate similar dissimilarities developing in the service sector. Accordingly, it might be useful to outline some of the possible causes of disparity, for, in general, they are barely touched upon in many texts.[2]

While precise definition of a service presents some difficulties due to lack of agreement as to what should be included/excluded for statistical purposes, there can be no doubt that the service sector is the largest and most important of most advanced economies. Recent data for the United Kingdom illustrate this point see Tables 8.1 and 8.2.

Not only is the service sector the largest in the economy, it is also the sector with the greatest growth potential and accounts for a disproportionately large share of any increase in consumers' discretionary purchasing power. Thus the service sector represents an attractive marketing opportunity, especially if it is amenable to the same scale economies as characterised the application of marketing technology to the sale of physical products.

However, as Stanton points out, 'Services possess distinctive characteristics which create marketing problems and result in marketing programs which are often substantially different from those found in the marketing of products.'[3] Among these characteristics Stanton singles out four for particular comment – intangibility, inseparability, heterogeneity, and perishability and fluctuating demand.

In essence it is a service's intangibility which distinguishes it from a physical product. Thus, while one can use objective criteria to describe the nature and performance of products, the same is only true to a limited extent of a service, for example, the value of an insurance policy on maturity, conditions or events under which it will mature, and so on. Clearly, the contention that customers are buying satisfactions or benefits becomes irrefutable in the case of services, and it may well transpire that the sellers of physical goods have as much to learn from the sellers of services when it comes to communicat-

TABLE 8.1 *Employees by industry group, 1972*

Industry type	Category	Number ('000s)	Percentage
Primary	Agriculture, forestry, fishing, mining and quarrying	427 ⎱ 379 ⎰	3·64
Secondary	Manufacturing	7778	35·17
	Construction	1300	5·88
Tertiary	Services*	12234	55·31
	TOTAL	22118	100

*Within the 'service' sector in the above table are included: gas, electricity and water supply, transportation, communication, the distributive trades, insurance, banking and finance, professional and scientific services, catering, national and local government services.

SOURCE: *Census of Employment.*

TABLE 8.2 *Gross domestic product by industry Group, 1972*
(£ million)

Industry type	Category	Value	Percentage
Primary	Agriculture, forestry, fishing, mining and quarrying	1541 ⎱ 827 ⎰	4·30
Secondary	Manufacturing	16645	30·22
	Construction	3432	6·23
Tertiary	Services*	32630	59·25
	TOTAL	55075	100

*See the note to Table 8.1

SOURCE: *National Income and Expenditure, 1973.*

ing a selling proposition as the latter have to learn from the former concerning other marketing techniques.

However, as indicated earlier, the transfer of marketing techniques has been delayed due to the *inseparability* of many services from the seller of the service, for example a haircut, beauty treatment, a taxi ride, car repairs, and so on and so forth. As a result of this personal involvement, the sale of many services has to be on a direct basis, which limits severely the scale of operation which is possible. On the other hand, many creators of services can employ agents to help improve their marketing coverage, an insurance agent, for example, while the package-tour brochure provides an excellent example of the application of advertising to create demand pull akin to that practised by many convenience-goods manufacturers.

A third factor which distinguishes many services is their heterogeneity, a natural outcome of the high level of personal involvement in the provision of such services. It is rather ironic that, while many manufacturers seek to differentiate their output to escape charges of homogeneity, it is the very lack of homogeneity which concerns many service organisations. For example, Stanton cites the uncertainty attached to many spectator sports concerning the standard or quality of the performance, while lack of consistency in repair services and transportation is a notable cause of customer complaint.

Finally, as Stanton points out, 'Services are highly perishable and they cannot be stored. Unused electrical power, empty seats in a stadium, and idle repairmen in a garage all represent business which is lost for ever. Furthermore, the market for services fluctuates considerably by seasons, by days of the week, and hours of the day.' It is this perishability and fluctuating demand which presents one of the greatest challenges to management in the creative combination of product planning, pricing and promotion functions to manipulate demand so that it corresponds more closely to the available supply. At first sight this may seem the very antithesis of the marketing-management concept, as it smacks of selling what one can make rather than making what one can sell. However, it is not difficult to see that by stimulating demand for under-utilised and perishable outputs, one is making a significant step towards maximising satisfaction from the use of scarce resources.

Although we suggested earlier that the delay in applying marketing ideas and techniques to the provision of services might be due, at least in part, to the more personal relationship between supplier and consumer, this is not to say that suppliers were truly customer-orientated. In fact, in many instances the reverse seems to have been (and still is) the case. Perhaps it is not without significance that several of the major examples cited by Theodore Levitt in his now classic 'Marketing Myopia'[4] were service industries. Thus the railroads failed because they conceived of themselves as being in the railroad business rather than in transportation: the movie business almost died because it ignored, then resisted, television, failing to see that films and television are both part of the entertainment business. Similarly, dry-cleaning, electric utilities and corner grocery stores have all suffered through a lack of sensitivity to customer needs.

Nowadays a similar problem seems to face many of the professions. Banking and insurance have gone some way towards catering to customer needs but still tend to adopt an approach which implies that they are doing you a favour by doing business with you, while their acolytes – accountants and solicitors – leave you in no doubt that this is the case. However, given present trends in consumer protection, there can be no doubt that unless these professions adopt a more sympathetic, dare one say marketing, approach to their clients, they are likely to find their monopolies exposed to close scrutiny and modification.

To sum up, the differences which distinguish services from products appear to be no greater nor more significant than those purported to differentiate between consumer and industrial goods. It follows, therefore, that the same principles and concepts should be of equal relevance to the marketing of services as to products notwithstanding the differences in degree and emphasis which will be called for. Thus the same sequence of market research, product/service planning and development, pricing, promotion, distribution, sale and after-sales service would seem to be equally appropriate to all marketing situations.

BROADENING THE MARKETING CONCEPT

If it is accepted that the same marketing approach is relevant to the sale of all goods and services, it does not seem a very big step to inquire whether the same philosophy and theory are not capable of still further extension to embrace all exchange relationships regardless of a cash or profit motivation. This very question provided the basis for a now famous article, 'Broadening the Concept of Marketing' by Kotler and Levy,[5] and has provided the foundation on which most subsequent discussion of the topic has been raised. Accordingly we consider it important to summarise and comment upon the main points made by Kotler and Levy.

The first point to be made is that most people regard marketing as a purely business activity involving functions such as product development, pricing, distribution and communication.

However, in Kotler and Levy's view, 'marketing is a pervasive societal activity that goes considerably beyond the selling of toothpaste, soap, and steel', an assertion which they support by citing the marketing of politicians and film stars, student recruitment by American universities, and the raising of money for 'causes'. But if one examines these latter activities one finds that little attention has been given them by marketers, save perhaps in the context of public relations, and that only as a relatively minor aspect of advertising. In Kotler and Levy's opinion such neglect is unforgivable for it threatens to relegate marketing permanently to a narrowly defined business activity and ignores the challenge and potential for extending marketing ideas into a much wider social framework.

In the preceding section we drew attention to the fact that the tertiary, or services, sector of our economy, like that of most, if not all, advanced industrialised economies, is now larger than both the primary and secondary sectors combined. However, in making this point we did not distinguish between business and non-business organisations, although the subsequent discussion focused upon services provided mainly by the former. Kotler and Levy suggest that, while business enterprises will remain a dominant form of organisation, other types of non-business organisation will become increasingly important. Major unions, religious organisations, government and local-government departments, universities, philanthropic foundations, hospitals, and the like, would all seem to fall into this category. Further, upon analysis it appears that all must perform the classic business functions – finance, procurement, production, personnel management and marketing. But, while the other business functions may be clearly identifiable, the marketing function is often not recognised explicitly as such.

As examples Kotler cites the 'community relations' programmes run by many police forces in the United States, as part of an effort to improve understanding between the police and the public, the Metropolitan Museum of Art's development of a series of 'happenings' designed to persuade citizens that museums are not dull, uninteresting mausoleums, the efforts of health educationists to promote the harmful effects of cigarette smoking and persuade people to give up the habit, and so on. Clearly all these activities have parallels in this and many other countries and lend substance to the claim that 'All of these organisations are concerned about their "product" in the eyes of certain "consumers" and are seeking to find "tools" for furthering their acceptance.'

Just as services may be viewed as intangible products, and so may be amenable to marketing techniques, as argued in the preceding pages, so too are ideas, organisations and persons. However, if we are to extend successfully the marketing concept to these areas it seems desirable that we should give some attention to defining profit (an aspect neglected by Kotler and Levy), for it appears that a source of considerable resistance in many non-business organisations to the transfer of ideas and techniques from the business sector are the undesirable connotations associated with money profits. Thus it seems that much ill-formed criticism is often directed toward the business sector because it measures performance in terms of monetary gains (and losses) which socially are ranked as inferior to more spiritual and possibly less tangible benefits. But, in the long run, it is clear that the only justification for any form of organisation is that it improves human welfare. Faced with limited resources, it seems reasonable to ask that we measure the performance of all types of activity so that we may concentrate our efforts upon those which add most to this over-all goal of maximising satisfaction. Accordingly, a concept of 'profit' or net surplus would seem to be just as appropriate in deciding priorities for education social welfare, health services, and the like, and organisations providing such services should be encouraged to grapple with the problems of defining and measuring their contribution to society. Clearly, a first step in such an effort must be a definition of the consumer need which is to be served and of the 'product' which will meet this need.

It should be stressed that the emphasis in the preceding sentence is rather different from that implied by the sequence – product, customer, tools – cited by Kotler and Levy, for this is a classical production orientation. If one is concerned with declining attendances in churches, with lack of enthusiasm for cultural opportunities provided by museums and art galleries, or lack of participation in the recreational activities offered by leisure centres, then the classical marketing approach of first identifying consumer needs and then relating them to the capabilities of the supplying organisation would seem to be the most important concept to communicate. Only if this is achieved is it likely that there will develop interest in marketing techniques, such as, for example, product-line pricing, or tools for dealing with problems of distribution and promotion.

In their analysis Kotler and Levy state that 'Nine concepts stand out as crucial in guiding the marketing effort of a business organisation.' They identify these as:

(1) Generic-product definition;
(2) Target-groups definition;
(3) Differentiated marketing;
(4) Customer-behaviour analysis;
(5) Differential advantages;
(6) Multiple marketing tools;
(7) Integrated marketing planning;
(8) Continuous marketing feedback;
(9) Marketing audit.

Most of these terms are well-known and understood by marketing practitioners, and do not merit elaboration here, although one example will help stimulate thought as to their relevance and transferability to a wider social context. Thus 'Churches at one time tended to define their product narrowly as that of producing religious services for members. Recently, most churchmen have decided that their basic product is human fellowship.'[6]

In our view, the major difficulty which faces any attempt to broaden the concept of marketing from the business to the non-business sector (sometimes referred to as 'meta marketing') lies not so much in demonstrating the utility of tools and techniques but in overcoming initial resistance to the materialistic connotation of 'marketing'. Perhaps one of our greatest weaknesses as practitioners is that we fail to practise what we preach and so tend to dismiss criticisms of marketing as ill-founded without considering that such expressed misgivings may be symptomatic of a much more radical concern and disillusionment, and, worse still, without doing very much to rectify what we regard as a misunderstanding of our true mission. In this belief we turn our attention in the next chapter to some of the main sources of criticism of marketing for until we understand our critics we would seem to have little chance of persuading them that the marketing concept can be extended to embrace other, non-business areas of human activity.

Chapter 9

Marketing under Attack[1]

Introduction

As indicated in the 'Preface', the thrust of this book has been concerned with establishing the need for a sound theoretical foundation on which to develop a discipline of marketing while recognising that the function and practice are of considerable antiquity. Based upon this argument we examined in Part 2 specific sub-areas within marketing to show how these had grown by borrowing concepts and ideas from other disciplines and then synthesising and developing these in a marketing context. And, in the preceding chapter, we reviewed the arguments in favour of extending the marketing concept into areas not traditionally associated with it – services and the outputs or 'products' of non-profit associations.

However, the title of this book is *Marketing: Theory and Practice*, and it would convey a false impression of the real-world situation if we were to close on a high point extolling the universality of marketing when it is quite clear that a number of serious reservations have been expressed concerning it. Accordingly, in this chapter we examine some of the major sources of marketing criticism.

Limitations of space preclude a full treatment of the multiplicity of sources of criticism, which Kotler[2] has classified into three main categories, namely

(1) *Marketing's impact on society:*
   (a) excessive materialism;
   (b) manipulation of demand;
   (c) neglect of social goods and costs;
   (d) cultural pollution;
   (e) excessive political power.
(2) *Marketing's impact on business competition:*
   (a) anti-competitive acquisition;

    (*b*) barriers to entry;
    (*c*) predatory competition.
  (3) *Marketing's impact on consumer welfare:*
    (*a*) high prices;
    (*b*) deceptive practices;
    (*c*) high-pressure selling;
    (*d*) shoddy or unsafe products;
    (*e*) planned obsolescence;
    (*f*) minority discrimination.

Kotler's treatment extends to a full chapter (22) of thirty-eight pages and is strongly recommended for study. For our part we must be content with a more condensed analysis of two issues (which are subsumed within Kotler's major categories) that are frequently raised as an argument against a marketing philosophy – convervation and consumerism.

    Conservation may be regarded as a general argument against a materialistic and consumption-dominated society which many consider to be synonymous with 'marketing', and will be discussed in the context of proposals for a zero-growth economy. Consumerism, for our purposes, will be reviewed as a particular example of focused and directed 'anti-marketing' thinking rather than in the all-embracing interpretation which includes conservation within it.

CONSERVATION AND MARKETING

At several points in this book we have adopted the economist's definition of the central problem facing world society as being 'maximising satisfaction from the utilisation of scarce resources'. Further, we have tended to emphasise maximising satisfaction, and have been critical of the economists' reluctance to incorporate subjective value judgements into concepts of choice and utility to any significant degree. In return, critics of marketing would argue that as a result of our emphasis upon satisfaction we tend to have lost sight of, or ignore, the constraint imposed upon consumption by the finite and scarce nature of many resources. In the early 1970s this scarcity has been brought home to the affluent economies of the world with great force as a result of the Arab oil embargo and the energy 'crisis' which it precipitated. Certainly this single event provided a focus for a growing body of opinion directed against conspicuous consumption, which it previously had lacked, for it had a direct effect upon the man in the street whereas concern about long-term exhaustion of physical resources lacked this impact.

To some degree the lack of impact of the conservationist argument may be attributed to the failure of Thomas Malthus's gloomy prognostications to come to pass during the early nineteenth century. In his *Essay on the Principle of Population* first published in 1798 Malthus advanced the proposition that population has a universal tendency to grow at a geometric progression. However, Malthus also pointed out that this tendency is subject to certain checks and, in the first edition, emphasised natural and positive limitations – disease, famine and war. (It is less well known that in the revised edition of his *Essay* Malthus took a less pessimistic view and acknowledged the possibility of preventive checks through what may be described broadly as 'family planning'.) While Malthus's ideas had enormous influence upon his contemporaries and are cited as 'the basis for a stern revision of the English poor laws',[3] and while he will always enjoy an honoured place in the annals of economic thought for his statement of the principle of diminishing returns, the essential concept he propounded lost influence due to its failure to materialise.

As Samuelson notes,

it is today recognised that his views were oversimplifications. In his discussion of diminishing returns, he never fully anticipated the miracles of the Industrial Revolution. In the next century technological innovation *shifted* production possibility curves *outward* and made possible better standards of living for more people. At the same time medical advances were prolonging human life and further lessening the positive checks to population. Nor did he realise that after 1870 in most Western nations, including the United States, family *fertility* as measured by actual number of children would begin to fall far short of family *fecundity*, or biological reproductive capacity.[4]

None of this is to suggest that the fundamental validity of Malthus's argument has ever been lost sight of, namely that there is a physical limit to the population which the world can

support. However, the advances due to technological innovation have tended to diminish sensitivity to this constraint until
the last two decades. In this latter period there has been a growing consciousness of our finite resource base which, in turn, has
led to growing dissatisfaction with the way in which we have been
using these resources; this has found expression in a number of
ways.

Perhaps the most influential statement of this view is that
contained in *The Limits to Growth*[5] which is an account of the
first phase of the Project on the Predicament of Mankind which
was sponsored by the Club of Rome 'in order to determine the
limits of the world system and the constraints which this
imposes upon population and consumption'.

Based upon its analysis of 'five major trends of global concern
– accelerating industrialisation, rapid population growth, widespread malnutrition, depletion of non-renewable resources, and
a deteriorating environment', the study team under Professor
Denis Meadows concluded that:

> If the present growth trends in world population, industrialis-
> ation, pollution, food production, and resource depletion
> continue unchanged, the limits to growth on this planet will
> be reached sometime within the next one hundred years. The
> most probable result will be a rather sudden and uncontrol-
> lable decline in both population and industrial capacity.

The team further concluded that it was possible to alter the
present trends and achieve a new equilibrium state, but that the
sooner work started, the better the chances of success. In grossly
simplified terms the remedy proposed is essentially a combination of population control and reduced consumption. While
there is not universal support for the Meadows model, nor for
the recommendations derived from it, there is a sufficient agreement to have given rise to what we term the 'zero-growth
syndrome'.

The Zero-Growth Syndrome

A major feature of the zero-growth syndrome is that it is anti-
new-product development. Such opposition is patently mis-
guided for it is clear that a very large proportion of all economic

growth during this century is the result of technological innovation rather than increases in factor inputs. It is also clear that a major stimulus to technological innovation is the reward of above-normal profit which can be earned through developing successful new products. The importance of innovation is implicit in many of Meadows's recommendations and more than explicit in the following quotation:

> Technological advance would be both necessary and welcome in the equilibrium state. A few obvious examples of the kinds of practical discovery that would enhance the workings of a steady state society include:
>
> New methods of waste collection, to decrease pollution and make discarded material available for recycling;
>
> More efficient techniques of recycling, to reduce rates of resource depletion;
>
> Better product design to increase product lifetime and promote easy repair, so that the capital depreciation rate would be minimised;
>
> Harnessing of incident solar energy, based on more complete understanding of ecological inter-relationships;
>
> Medical advances that would decrease the death rate;
>
> Contraceptive advances that would facilitate the equalisation of the birth rate with the decreasing death rate.

It is clear that there is ample scope for innovation and new-product development in achieving and maintaining the desired steady state. Thus the criticism would seem to be directed not so much at the actual processes of new-product development but rather at some of its manifestations. Of these perhaps the most frequently criticised aspects are those embraced by the phrases 'product proliferation', 'planned obsolescence' and 'conspicuous consumption'.

Marketing and Materialism

While it would be naive to deny that marketing must bear some responsibility for all of these undesirable facets of modern society, it would be equally naive to accept all the blame. We have already expressed the view that a central feature of marketing is that it seeks to measure consumer preferences and then satisfy them. If much of modern society is materialistic it should be remembered that materialism is not a new state – the only salient difference between twentieth-century materialism and that of previous centuries is that the condition is much more widespread now than hitherto. No longer is non-essential consumption the prerogative of the upper and middle classes – in the advanced economies it is the privilege of virtually all, and few would claim that increased consumption and the enhanced standard of living it confers is bad.

It would seem, therefore, that the criticism is directed at excessive consumption, not at improved consumption. However as we have already suggested, marketing reflects society's wishes as much as it conditions and moulds them. Ever since the depression of the late 1920s and early 1930s the economic policy of most western economies has been based upon the thinking of John Maynard Keynes. It was Keynes who postulated that a major cause of the depression and the unemployment which accompanied it was underconsumption. The Protestant Ethic extols the virtue of labour, so clearly the aim of government policy must be to stimulate consumption, for this will increase the demand for labour and alleviate the indignity of unemployment. This is admittedly a rather trite synopsis of economic thinking over the past thirty years or so, but there can be no denying that the maintenance of full employment has been a central plank in the platform of all political parties at all general elections ever since the Beveridge Report of 1944.

The deficiency of this economic policy is very similar to the deficiency of the production- and sales-management orientations which preceded marketing as a managerial philosophy – all tend to stress quantity rather than quality. It would be more than invidious to blame business for implementing government, and therefore presumably society's, wishes in pursuing an expansionist policy, but this is just what we are in danger of doing. If, as now seems to be the case, we are more concerned with the conservation of resources than with their accelerated consumption, it would be more constructive if we were to allow management time in which to develop new policies and redeploy resources accordingly. Certainly it will take a long time to re-educate consumers to prefer durability to novelty and quality to quantity.

However, if it is necessary to re-educate consumers to prefer more durable products, to accept protein substitutes for fresh meat, to run smaller cars, to practise birth control, in fact to adopt willingly any significant change in their behaviour and/or consumption patterns, then surely marketing techniques will have a major role to play.

THE IMPACT OF CONSUMERISM

Although it is often erroneously assumed that the consumerist movement owes its existence to the growth of conspicuous consumption in the 1950s and 1960s, and the reaction to it implicit in the writings of Vance Packard,[6] Rachel Carson[7] and Ralph Nader,[8] there appears to be a fundamental paradox in the apparent conflict between two activities – consumerism and marketing – both of which claim that their central interest is maximising consumer satisfaction. However, a moment's reflection suggests that perhaps this seeming inconsistency is less contradictory than might appear at first sight.

As we have implied in the preceding paragraph, consumerism is no more an invention of the twentieth century than is marketing. Marketing has existed ever since man perceived the advantages to be gained from job specialisation, for, while such specialisation results in marked increases in productivity, it also creates the need for exchange so that individual producers may acquire products other than those which they make themselves. But as soon as men begin to enter into exchange relationships it becomes clear that there is a need for some system of rules to govern the nature of transactions, for, otherwise, the less scrupulous will take advantage of the customers with weak bargaining power. The protection of consumer interest is central to the consumerist movement so perhaps we should consider it unsurprising that increases in the level of marketing activity should be paralleled by an increase in activities designed to protect consumers.

For example, the growth of the medieval craft guilds resulted in a considerable increase in the supply of goods, and also resulted in the promulgation of devices to protect the consumer, for example the hallmarking of precious metals, as well as the evolution of voluntary codes of practice to govern standards of manufacture and trading. At the same time, certain common-law principles were evolved for the protection of both seller and buyer, such as the ruling that stolen goods purchased in market overt could not be recovered by their original owner. At a time when virtually all transactions took place in the open, and products lacked the homogeneity associated with mass production, such that individual goods might be readily identified, it seemed reasonable that one should acquire good title if buying stolen goods in the open market and in good faith. Under today's trading conditions the owners of stolen goods cannot be expected to have the same opportunity to recover their own property, and it has been necessary to change the law to reflect the changed situation. Similarly, the inherent complexity of many products, and of the distribution channels through which they pass between producer and consumer, demand modifications of earlier legislation designed to protect the consumer, such as the Sale of Goods Act of 1893.

At the present time, the consumerist lobby represents only a small proportion of all consumers, both here, in the United States and in Europe. However, it is a very vocal and influential minority that has secured considerable success in persuading governments to enact legislation to improve the users' bargaining power and to protect them against misleading marketing practices. In the United Kingdom it is widely accepted that the consumerist movement is predominantly middle class (as the nature of the products reviewed in *Which* clearly indicates), and that while its concern is with value for money its definition of value is essentially objective, and neglects, ignores and sometimes actively disapproves of any suggestion of subjective values created by promotional activity. None the less, active consumerists represent a sufficiently large market segment to warrant very close attention as a market opportunity. Moreover, unlike most market segments, consumerists are unusually articulate in spelling out exactly what it is they are looking for in terms of acceptable product specifications. Thus we would argue that consumerists represent a worthwhile marketing opportunity in their own right. If the consumerists' concern with brand proliferation, planned obsolescence, after-sales service, truth in advertising and lending, bio-degradable packaging and so on and so forth, represents the thinking of all consumers ten years from now, then there would seem to be very significant advantages in evaluating the precise nature of the consumerist demands and the development of goods and services to meet these demands today, for it will give the alert manufacturer ample opportunity to test-market a new strategy for prospering under these changed conditions.

In short, we return to our argument that the function of marketing is to maximise consumer satisfaction at a profit. If consumer demand changes then marketing should be the first to sense the nature and direction of this change and modify its own policies and practices accordingly. There is no fundamental conflict between consumerism and marketing – their basic objective is the same.

MARKETING AND INFLATION

Earlier in this chapter we suggested that the 'energy crisis' provided a focus for a rather diffuse body of opinion with the common feature that it was concerned with the irresponsible manner in which society was consuming scarce resources. We also suggested that this focus arose very largely from the fact that the consequences of the energy crisis had a direct and immediate effect upon the man in the street and so sensitised him to the validity of the conservationist's argument. As the citizens of most of the world's economies are aware, the consequence of the energy crisis has been inflation – a condition which many argue is the direct result of excessive consumption. Marketing is frequently viewed as a consumption-orientated activity; therefore one solution to our problems is 'stop marketing'.

More specifically, inflation is seen as the direct consequence of an excess demand for goods and services, with the result that too much money is chasing too few goods. Given such a situation, we do not need to have taken a course in advanced economics to appreciate that the most likely outcome, at least in the short term, is an increase in price. After all, the function of the market is to equate demand and supply at an equilibrium price.

In fact the 'demand-pull' school of thought represents only one interpretation of the causes of inflation – the other most frequently cited causes being 'cost-push' and 'monetary' inflation. In simple terms, cost-push inflation is set in train when some groups of workers secure a substantial pay increase which leads in turn to an increase in the costs and price of their output. Consumers of the firm's output, faced with an increase in the cost of living and wishing to maintain parity of earnings with those who have just won a rise, put in their own claim. Further, in an inflationary situation, the second group of workers fear that by the time their claim is settled it will have been eroded by other price increases and taxation, and so will press for significantly more than they would be prepared to accept under more stable conditions. This escalation of wage claims gives rise to a wage–price spiral in which the increase in the volume of money outstrips increases in the volume of goods and services available for consumption, and, once again, leads to too much money chasing too few goods.

An increase in the money supply is also viewed as the third main cause of inflation – 'monetary' inflation. However, in the case of monetary inflation, the catalyst which initiates the inflationary spiral is an increase in the quantity of money rather than an increase in wages and costs. Such increases in the money supply usually take place when government exceeds its ability to raise revenue through increased taxes or borrowing and so must resort to printing more bank-notes in order to cover its commitments. Unfortunately, such increases in the money supply usually outstrip any increases in productivity, resulting once again in too much money chasing too few goods.

While these are grossly oversimplified representations of three main schools of thought concerning the causes of inflation, none the less they suffice to convey the basic point that a significant increase in the supply of money (or a significant decline in the supply of goods) will result in a rise in price, or, put another way, a decline in purchasing power. On a limited scale and in the short term, such fluctuations are to be expected and are no cause for concern. But, if they lead to a loss of confidence in the value of money, they set in train a vicious spiral of present consumption, rather than deferred consumption in the form of investment and saving, which accelerates price increases and wage demands designed to offset such price increases.

As noted earlier, critics of marketing are really supporters of the demand-pull school and so would seem to argue for the remedies appropriate to such inflation – a reduction in private purchasing power through higher taxes and credit restrictions, as well as a cut-back in public expenditure upon socially desirable projects such as schools, hospitals and other forms of social and welfare benefit. (In passing, one might observe that present stocks of cars and under-utilised capacity in many industries reflect excess supply rather than excess demand.) Of course, such policies are equally appropriate to cost-push inflation, although in this instance they are likely to be termed 'wage and price control'. Given this degree of similarity between the different forms of inflation and their cures, it seems reasonable to ask why marketing should be singled out for blame rather than, for example, restrictive-labour practices, insufficient investment in innovation, or simple bone-idleness. Without wishing to claim that marketing is wholly without fault, it would seem more constructive to recognise that our poor economic performance is the result of a combination of interdependent factors which need to be treated together.

SUMMARY

In this chapter we have looked briefly at three sources of economic and social concern which have prompted observers to question the relevance of marketing. We have argued that these three sources of criticism – consumerism, inflation and the zero-growth syndrome – all spring from the same origin, a realisation that a continuation of present consumption patterns and trends is likely to result in exhaustion of the world's finite resources in the not too distant future.

We have suggested that marketing has been singled out for particular criticism on the grounds that it is frequently viewed as synonymous with demand stimulation, and excess demand is seen as the root cause of the projected disequilibrium. It is unnecessary to deny that demand stimulation is marketing's prime objective (although most marketers would, in fact, do so) in order to reject this criticism, for it would only be tenable if marketing's efforts to stimulate demand were concerned solely with *volume*. As all true marketing men know, marketing's prime preoccupation is maximising consumer satisfaction at a profit acceptable to the supplier – a point made forcibly by the British Printing Industries Federation in its magazine *Printing Industries*. For example, it was reported that

Printers cannot hope for better returns on capital when they are forced to lower prices merely to retain their present customers. In future they will have to rely on better marketing. . . . The federation said printers should realise that better marketing was not necessarily concerned with selling the maximum volume at the lowest price to the greatest number of customers. *It might equally be selling the best at the highest price to a minority* [our emphasis].[9]

The report continued: 'In the present difficult times, member firms need to be quite a lot more profitable merely in order to survive.' Improved marketing is suggested as the appropriate remedy.

It is our view that there is no fundamental inconsistency between marketing and economic and social objectives – an improvement in the standard of living and the general quality of life in general – even though the means of achieving these are subject to reconsideration at the present time. Rather, we view marketing as the business discipline best equipped to cope with such change, starting as it does with planning in order to determine the nature of consumer needs and then co-operating with all the other business functions to ensure that customers receive the right product at the right place, price and time. Further, if there is a need to educate people as to the need for conservation rather than conspicuous consumption, marketing and advertising men are probably better equipped to communicate this message than most other people. (Clearly a significant contributory factor to the present inflationary situation is a loss of consumer confidence – building consumer confidence is a major marketing activity.)

However, it also seems to us that marketing men must be prepared to stand up and be counted, and to use the skills they deploy so effectively in selling goods and services to communicate the relevance and value of marketing to the general public. If we fail to do this then perhaps marketing does not deserve a future.

Notes and References

Chapter 1

1. Philip Kotler, *Marketing Management*, 2nd edn (Englewood Cliffs, N.J.: Prentice-Hall, 1972), p. 6.
2. This follows a trichotomy suggested by Robert L. King in 'The Marketing Concept', in *Science in Marketing*, ed. George Schwartz (New York: Wiley, 1965). The discussion on these different orientations draws extensively on this source.
3. See *World Dynamics* (Cambridge, Mass.: Wright-Allen Press, 1971).
4. D. Meadows *et al.*, *The Limits to Growth* (London: Earth Island, 1972).
5. King, 'The Marketing Concept'.
6. *Marketing*, 2nd edn (London: Macmillan, 1974), pp. 26 ff.
7. Quoted from an unpublished paper, 'The Marketing Concept in General Electric', by Edward S. McKay.
8. General Electric Company, *Annual Report, 1952*.
9. 'An Interpretation of the Marketing Concept', *Advancing Marketing Efficiency*, Proceedings of the 41st National Conference, American Marketing Association (Chicago, 1959), cited in King, 'The Marketing Concept'.
10. See, for example, Vance Packard's books, *The Hidden Persuaders* (London: Longmans, Green, 1957) and *The Waste Makers* (London: Longmans, Green, 1961). Also Ralph Nader's *Unsafe at any Speed* (New York: Grossman, 1963).
11. Lawrence Abbott, *Quality and Competition* (Columbia University Press, 1955).

Chapter 2

1. Michael Halbert, *The Meaning and Sources of Marketing Theory* (New York: McGraw-Hill, 1965).
2. *Harvard Business Review* (Jan.–Feb. 1963).
3. 'The Hunting of Advertising Effectiveness', reprinted in *Admap* (Feb 1975).

4. 'Towards an Alternative Advertising Theory', *Admap* (Jan 1974).

5. *Marketing in a Competitive Economy* (London: Hutchinson, 1965).

Chapter 3

1. *The Meaning and Sources of Marketing Theory* (New York: McGraw-Hill, 1965).

2. *Journal of Marketing*, vol. 32 (Jan 1968) pp. 29–33.

3. See particularly *The Development of Marketing Thought* (Homewood, Ill.: Irwin, 1962) and his contribution to *Science in Marketing*, ed. George Schwartz (New York: Wiley, 1965).

4. Arch. W. Shaw, 'Some Problems in Marketing Distribution', *Quarterly Journal of Economics* (Aug 1912); L. D. H. Weld, 'Marketing Functions and Mercantile Organisation', *American Economic Review* (June 1917); and Paul T. Cherington, *The Elements of Marketing* (London: Macmillan, 1920).

5. *Retail Selling and Store Management* (New York: D. Appleton Century, 1913) and *The Economics of Retailing* (New York: Ronald Press, 1915).

6. Halbert, *The Meaning and Sources of Marketing Theory*, pp. 63–4.

7. Ibid.

8. Ibid. p. 24.

9. Ibid. p. 127.

Chapter 4

1. George Katona, *The Powerful Consumer* (New York: McGraw-Hill, 1960).

2. George Katona, *The Mass Consumption Society* (New York: McGraw-Hill, 1964).

3. Andrew Shonfield, 'Neglect of Psychology in Managing the Economy', *The Times* (24 Feb 1971).

4. G. W. Allport, *The Nature of Prejudice* (Reading, Mass.: Addison-Wesley, 1954).

5. See Philip Kotler, *Marketing Management: Analysis, Planning and Control* (Englewood Cliffs, N.J.: Prentice-Hall, 1967).

6. Ibid.

7. Ibid.

8. See C. Glenn Walters, *Consumer Behavior: Theory and Practice* (Glencoe, Ill.: Irwin, 1974).

9. Kotler, *Marketing Management: Analysis, Planning and Control.*

10. Alfred Marshall, *Principles of Economics* (London: Macmillan, 1927).

11. Francesco M. Nicosia, *Consumer Decision Processes: Marketing and Advertising Implications* (Englewood Cliffs, N.J.: Prentice-Hall, 1966).

12. See Walters, *Consumer Review.*

13. James F. Engel, David T. Kollat and Roger D. Blackwell, *Consumer Behavior* (New York: Holt, Rinehart & Winston, 1968).

14. Joseph Clawson, 'Lewin's Psychology and Motives in Marketing' in *Theory in Marketing*, ed. R. Cox and W. Alderson (Glencoe, Ill.: Irwin, 1950).

15. John A. Howard and Jagdish N. Sheth, *The Theory of Buyer Behavior* (New York: Wiley, 1969).

16. Allport, *The Nature of Prejudice.*

17. David B. Montgomery and Glen L. Urban, *Management Science in Marketing* (Englewood Cliffs, N.J.: Prentice-Hall, 1969).

18. W. T. Tucker, 'Consumer Research: Status and Prospects', in *Consumer Behavior: Contemporary Research in Action*, ed. Robert J. Holloway, Robert A. Mittelstaedt and M. Ventaktesan (Boston: Houghton Mifflin, 1971).

19. John U. Farley and L. Winston Ring, 'An Empirical Test of the Howard–Sheth Model of Buyer Behaviour', *Journal of Marketing Research* (Nov 1970).

20. Bernard Berelson and Gary A. Steiner, *Human Behavior: An Inventory of Scientific Findings* (New York: Harcourt, Brace & World, 1963).

21. Peter J. McClure and John K. Ryans, 'Differences Between Retailers' and Consumers' Perceptions', *Journal of Marketing Research* (Feb 1968).

22. Milton Blum and Valentine Appel, 'Consumer versus Management Reaction in New Package Development', *Journal of Applied Psychology* (Aug 1961).

23. James C. Makens, 'Effect of Brand Preference upon Consumers' Perceived Taste of Turkey Meat', *Journal of Applied Psychology* (Aug 1965).

24. Robert L. Brown, 'Wrapper Influence on the Perception of Freshness in Bread', *Journal of Applied Psychology* (Aug 1958).

25. Mason Haire, 'Projective Techniques in Marketing Research', *Journal of Marketing* (1950).

26. Raymond A. Bauer and Stephen Greyser, *Advertising in America: The Consumer View*, Division of Research, Graduate School of Business Administration, Harvard University (1968).

27. Berelson and Steiner, *Human Behavior*.

28. James H. Myers and William Reynolds, *Consumer Behavior and Marketing Management* (Boston: Houghton Mifflin, 1967).

29. Herbert E. Krugman, 'The Learning of Consumer Preference', *Journal of Marketing* (Apr 1962).

30. Donald F. Cox, 'Clues for Advertising Strategists', *Harvard Business Review*, pt I (Sep–Oct 1961) pt II (Nov–Dec 1961).

31. Leo Bogart, *Strategy in Advertising* (New York: Harcourt, Brace & World, 1967).

32. T. S. Robertson, *Consumer Behavior* (Glenview, Ill.: Scott, Foresman & Co., 1970).

33. Ibid.

34. Carl I. Hovland, Irving L. Janis and Harold H. Kelley, *Communication and Persuasion* (Yale University Press, 1953).

35. Bogart, *Strategy in Advertising*.

36. Benton J. Underwood, 'Interference and Forgetting', *Psychological Review*, vol. 64 (1957).

37. Alfred A. Kuehn, 'Consumer Brand Choice as a Learning Process', *Journal of Advertising Research* (Dec 1962).

38. Calvin S. Hall and Gardner Lindzey, *Theories of Personality* (New York: Wiley, 1957).

39. Berelson and Steiner, *Human Behavior*.

40. Tucker, 'Consumer Research: Status and Prospects'.

41. Robert P. Brody and Scott M. Cunningham, 'Personality Variables and the Consumer Decision Process', *Journal of Marketing Research* (Feb 1968).

42. Nicosia, *Consumer Decision Processes*.

43. Gardner Lindzey, *Assessment of Human Motives* (New York: Holt, Rinehart & Winston, 1960).

44. Ernest Dichter, *Handbook of Consumer Motivations* (New York: McGraw-Hill, 1964).

45. Harry Henry, *Motivation Research* (London: Crosby, Lockwood & Son Ltd, 1963).

46. Martin Fishbein, *Attitude Theory and Measurement* (New York: Wiley, 1967).

47. M. Bird and A. S. C. Ehrenberg, 'Consumer Attitudes and Brand Usage', *Journal of the Market Research Society* (1970).

48. William D. Barclay, 'The Semantic Differential as an Index of Brand Attitude', *Journal of Advertising Research* (Mar 1964).

49. Jon G. Udell, 'Can Attitude Measurement Predict Consumer Behavior?', *Journal of Marketing* (Oct 1965).

50. Irving S. White, 'The Functions of Advertising in Our Culture', *Journal of Marketing* (July 1959).

51. Joseph A. Kahl, *The American Class Structure* (New York: Holt, Rinehart & Winston, 1957).

52. Stuart U. Rich and Subhash C. Jain, 'Social Class and Life Cycle as Predictors of Shopping Behavior', *Journal of Marketing Research* (Feb 1968).

53. Pierre D. Martineau, 'The Pattern of Social Classes', in *Proceedings of the American Marketing Association*, ed. Robert L. Clewett (1957).

54. Sidney J. Levy, 'Social Class and Consumer Behavior', in *On Knowing the Consumer*, ed. Joseph W. Newman (New York: Wiley, 1966).

55. Sidney J. Levy and Ira O. Glick, *Living with Television* (Chicago: Aldine, 1962).

56. Solomon E. Asch, 'Effects of Group Pressure upon the Modification and Distortion of Judgments' in *Readings in Social Psychology*, ed. Eleanor E. Maccoby (New York: Holt, Rinehart & Winston, 1958).

57. M. Venkatesan, 'Experimental Study of Consumer Behavior, Conformity and Independence', *Journal of Marketing Research* (November 1966).

58. James E. Stafford, 'Effects of Group Influences on Consumer Brand Preferences', *Journal of Marketing Research* (Feb 1966).

Chapter 5

1. Indeed the use of the phraseology 'target market' reflects early 'propagandist' interpretations of the effect of persuasive communication. Under this interpretation the audience is viewed as so many passive targets waiting to be 'hit' by the advertisement or contacted by the salesman etc.

2. S. H. Britt, 'Are So-Called Successful Advertising Campaigns Really Successful?', *Journal of Advertising Research*, vol. 9, no. 2 (1969).

3. See, for example, L. Festinger, *A Theory of Cognitive Dissonance* (New York: Harper, 1957) for the theoretical background to this position and R. J. Holloway, 'An Experiment on Consumer Dissonance', *Journal of Marketing*, vol. 31 (Jan 1969) for an example of its application.

4. R. J. Lavidge and G. A. Steiner, 'A Model for Predictive Measurement of Advertising Effectiveness', *Journal of Marketing* (25 Oct 1961).

5. For a review see E. M. Rogers and T. F. Shoemaker, *Communication of Innovations* (Glencoe, Ill.: Free Press, 1971).

6. S. Pollit, 'Has Anything Gone Wrong with Advertising Research?', *Admap* (May 1971).

7. S. Moscovici, 'Attitudes and Opinions', *Annual Review of Psychology*, 14 (1963) pp. 249–50.

8. E. Katz and P. F. Lazarsfeld, *Personal Influence: The Part Played by People in the Flow of Mass Communications* (New York: Free Press, 1955).

9. Ibid.

10. B. Ryan and N. Gross, 'The Diffusion of Hybrid Seed Corn in Two Iowa Communities', *Rural Sociology*, VIII (Mar 1943) pp. 15–24.

11. Reviewed by Rogers and Shoemaker, *Communication of Innovations*.

12. W. Schramm, 'How Communication Works', in *The Process and Effects of Mass Communication*, 6th edn, ed. W. Schramm (University of Illinois Press, 1965).

13. R. A. Bauer, 'The Role of the Audience in the Communication Process: Summary', in *Proceedings of the American Marketing Association*, ed. Stephen A. Greyser, American Marketing Association, Chicago (1963).

14. J. T. Klapper, *The Effects of Mass Communication* (New York: Free Press, 1960).

15. C. I. Hovland, I. L. Janis and H. H. Kelley, *Communication and Persuasion* (Yale University Press, 1953).

16. Klapper, *Effects of Mass Communication*.

17. D. A. Fuchs, 'Two Source Effects in Magazine Advertising', *Journal of Marketing Research* (Aug 1964) pp. 59–62.

18. Katz and Lazarsfeld, *Personal Influence*.

19. Hovland, Janis and Kelley, *Communication and Persuasion*.

20. Klapper, *Effects of Mass Communication*.

21. C. W. King and J. O. Summers, *Interaction Patterns in Interpersonal Communication*, paper no. 168, West Lafayette, Indiana, Herman C. Krannert Graduate School of Industrial Administration, Purdue University Institute for Research in the Behavioral, Economic and Management Sciences (1967).

22. E. M. Rogers, *Diffusion of Innovations* (New York: Free Press, 1962).

23. Klapper, *Effects of Mass Communication*.

24. See C. W. King and J. O. Summers, 'Overlap of Opinion Leadership across Consumers' Product Categories', *Journal of Marketing Research*, vol. 7 (Feb 1970).

25. Katz and Lazarsfeld, *Personal Influence*.

26. Rogers, *Diffusion of Innovations*.

27. J. R. Mancuso, 'Why Not Create Opinion Leaders for New Product Introductions?', *Journal of Marketing*, vol. 33 (July 1969) pp. 20–5.

28. See, for example, F. E. Webster, 'Informal Communication in

Industrial Markets, *Journal of Marketing Research* (May 1970) pp. 186–9, and J. Martilla, 'Word of Mouth Communication in the Industrial Adoption Process', *Journal of Marketing Research*, vol. VIII (May 1971) pp. 173–8.

29. R. Bauer, 'Consumer Behavior as Risk Taking', in *Proceedings of the 43rd National Conference of the American Marketing Association*, ed. R. S. Hancock, A.M.A., Chicago (1963).

30. See, for example, D. F. Cox, 'Information and Uncertainty: Their Effects on the Consumers' Product Evaluations', Boston H. B. School D.B.A. Thesis (1963); and J. Arndt, 'Perceived Risk, Sociometric Integration and Word of Mouth Advertising in the Adoption of a New Product', in *Science Technology and Marketing*, ed. R. M. Haas, Proceedings of the American Marketing Association, Chicago (1966) pp. 698–721.

31. G. S. Day, 'Attitude Change, Media and Word of Mouth', *Journal of Advertising Research*, II (6) (1971).

32. I. L. Janis and S. Feshbach, 'Effects of Fear-Arousing Communications', *Journal of Abnormal and Social Psychology*, vol. 48 (Jan 1953) pp. 78–92.

33. For a review see K. L. Higbee, 'Fifteen Years of Fear Arousal: Research on Threat Appeals, 1953–1968', *Psychological Bulletin*, vol. 72.

34. M. L. Ray and W. L. Wilkie, 'Fear: The Potential of an Appeal Neglected by Marketing', *Journal of Marketing*, vol. 34 (Jan 1970) pp. 54–62.

35. For a review see I. L. Janis, 'Effects of Fear Arousal on Attitude Change: Recent Developments in Theory and Experimental Research', *Advances in Experimental Social Psychology*, vol. 3 (1967) pp. 167–225.

36. H. Ebinghauss, *Das Gedachtnis* (Berlin: Duncker & Humbolt, 1885).

37. An up-to-date review is given by M. L. Ray, A. G. Sawyer and E. C. Strong, 'Frequency Effects Revisited', *Journal of Advertising Research*, vol. II no. 1 (Feb 1971). The classic paper remains that of H. A. Zielske, 'The Remembering and Forgetting of Advertising', *Journal of Marketing* (Jan 1959).

38. H. Claychamp and A. Amstutz, 'Simulation Techniques in the Analysis of Market Strategy', in *Applications of the Sciences in Marketing Management*, ed. Frank M. Bass (New York: Wiley, 1968) pp. 113–51.

Chapter 6

1. A. Marshall, *Economics of Industry*, IV (London: Macmillan, 1898).

2. W. Alderson and M. W. Martin, 'Towards a Formal Theory of Transactions and Transvections', *Journal of Marketing Research* (May 1965).

3. W. Alderson, 'Factors Governing the Development of Marketing Channels', in *Marketing Channels for Manufactured Products* (Glencoe, Ill.: Irwin, 1954).

4. Ibid.

5. Alderson and Martin, 'Towards a Formal Theory of Transactions and Transvections'.

6. L. P. Bucklin, *Theory of Distribution Channel Structures* (Berkeley: Institute of Business and Economic Research, University of California, 1966) p. 107.

7. M. Smith, *Retail Distribution* (Oxford University Press, 1937) ch. VI.

8. P. Ford, 'Excessive Competition in the Retail Trade, 1901–1931', *Economic Journal*, vol. XLV (1935) pp. 501–8.

9. Marshall, *Economics of Industry*.

10. M. Hall and J. Knapp, 'Gross Margins and Efficiency Measurement in the Retail Trade', *Oxford Economic Papers*, vol. 7 (1955) pp. 312–36.

11. S. Pollard and J. D. Hughes, 'Retailing Costs, Some Comments on the Census of Distribution 1950', *Oxford Economic Papers*, vol. 7 (1955) pp. 71–93.

12. K. D. George and P. V. Hills, *Productivity and Capital Expenditure in Retailing*, Occasional Paper No. 16, University of Cambridge (1968).

13. W. B. Reddaway, *Effects of Selective Employment Tax. First Report: The Distributive Trades* (London: H.M.S.O., 1970).

14. Smith, *Retail Distribution*, ch. IV.

15. E. H. Chamberlain, *Towards a more General Theory of Value* (Oxford University Press, 1957) p. 47.

16. M. P. McNair, *Significant Trends and Developments in the Post War Period in Competitive Distribution in a High Level Economy* (Pittsburgh University Press, 1958).

17. *The Distributive Trades in the Common Market* (Distributive Trades, Economic Development Committee, 1973).

18. L. P. Bucklin, *Competition and Evolution in the Distributive Trades* (Englewood Cliffs, N.J.: Prentice-Hall, 1972) pp. 123–5.

19. D. Metcalf, 'Concentration in the Retail Grocery Industry in Great Britain', *Farm Economist,* vol. 11 (1968) pp. 294–303.

20. B. C. McCammon, 'Alternative Explanations of Institutional Change', in *Towards Scientific Marketing,* ed. Stephen A. Greyser, Proceedings of The American Marketing Association (Chicago, 1963).

21. P. McAnally, *Economics of the Distributive Trades* (London: Allen & Unwin, 1971) p. 34.

22. W. J. Reilly, *The Law of Retail Gravitation* (New York: Putnam, 1931).

23. P. D. Converse, 'New Laws of Retail Gravitation', *Journal of Marketing* (Jan 1949).

24. D. L. Huff, 'Defining and Estimating a Trading Area', *Journal of Marketing* (July 1964).

25. T. R. Lakshamanan and W. G. Hansen, 'A Retail Market Potential Model', *Journal of the American Institute of Planners* (May 1965).

26. D. Thorpe and T. C. Rhodes, 'The Shopping Centres of the Tyneside Urban Region', *Economic Geography,* vol. 42 (1966).

27. G. Heald, 'The Application of AID Programme and Multiple Regression Techniques to the Assessment of Store Performance and Site Selection', *Operation Research Quarterly,* no. 20 (1972).

28. D. W. Greeno, M. S. Sommers and J. B. Kernan, 'Personality and Implicit Behaviour Patterns', *Journal of Marketing Research* (Feb 1973) pp. 63–9.

29. J. A. Lunn, 'Psychological Classifications', *Commentary* (July 1966).

30. D. Beazley, Shopping Styles and Strategies and their Relationship to In-Store Factors', *Management Information for Retail Organisations,* Proceedings of ESOMAR seminar (Apr 1974).

31. A. Thabor, 'Marketing Information and Simulation Systems for a French Retailers Chain', in ibid.

32. *Merchandising Characteristics of Grocery Store Commodities* (U.S. Department of Commerce, 1929), *General Foods Study* (McKinsey, 1963); R. C. Curham, 'Shelf Space Allocation and Profit Maximisation in Mass Retailing', *Journal of Marketing* (July 1973).

33. 'Towards a Formal Theory of Transactions and Tranvsections'.

34. L. P. Bucklin, 'Postponement, Speculation and the Structure of Distribution Channels', *Journal of Marketing Research* (Feb 1965).

35. See H. H. Baligh and L. E. Richartz, *Vertical Market Structures* (Boston: Allyn & Bacon, 1967).

36. See M. Hall, *Distributive Trading* (London: Hutchinson, 1950) ch. v, pp. 75–88.

37. See F. F. Balderston, 'Communications Networks in Intermediate Markets', *Management Science,* IV (Jan 1958).

38. *Competition and Evolution in the Distributive Trades.*

39. Ibid.

40. See N. A. H. Stacey and A. Wilson, *The Changing Pattern of Distribution* (Oxford: Pergamon, 1965).

41. J. B. Jeffreys, *The Distribution of Consumer Goods* (Cambridge University Press, 1950).

42. R. Cox and C. S. Goodman, 'Marketing of Housebuilding Materials', *Journal of Marketing* (July 1956).

43. P. Rosson, 'Changing Traditional Distribution Systems', *International Journal of Physical Distribution*, vol. 4, no. 5, pp. 305–16.

44. L. P. Bucklin, 'The Classification of Channel Structures', in *Vertical Marketing Systems*, ed. Bucklin (Glenview, Ill.: Scott, Foresman, 1970).

45. L. E. Gill, 'A Graphic Interpretation of Distribution Channel Structures', Ph.D. thesis (Ohio State University, 1968).

46. 'The Classification of Channel Structures.'

47. See M. J. Baker and A. J. Brown, *The Marketing of Meat in Europe* (University of Strathclyde, 1974).

48. J. K. Galbraith and R. H. Holton, *Marketing Efficiency in Puerto Rico* (Harvard University Press, 1955).

49. C. C. Slater, 'Market Channel Co-ordination and Economic Development', in *Vertical Marketing Systems*, ed. Bucklin.

50. L. E. Richartz, 'A Game Theoretic Formulation of Vertical Market Structures', in *Vertical Marketing Systems*, ed. Bucklin.

51. See F. M. Jones, 'A New Interpretation of Marketing Functions', *Journal of Marketing* (Jan 1943); and H. Bund and Carroll, 'The Changing Role of the Marketing Function', *Journal of Marketing* (Jan 1957).

52. *Vertical Market Structures.*

53. See F. Wentworth (ed.), *Physical Distribution Management* (Gower Press, 1970); and G. Brice (ed.), *The International Journal of Physical Distribution Bibliography 1965–73 for Institute of Scientific Business.*

54. J. C. Heskitt, 'Sweeping Changes in Distribution', *Harvard Business Review* (Mar–Apr 1973) p. 123.

55. See B. T. Bayliss and S. L. Edwards, *Industrial Demand for Transport* (Ministry of Transport, 1970); and A. J. Brown, 'Variables affecting the choice of Distribution Channels', in *International Journal of Physical Distribution*, no. 5, (1974).

56. See Department of Trade and Industry, *The Costing of Handling and Storage in Warehouses* (H.M.S.O., 1970).

57. See R. Artle and S. Berglund, 'A Note on Manufacturer's Choice of Distribution Channels', *Management Science* (July 1959).

58. *Vertical Market Structures.*

59. See D. Moore, *Costing for Marketing Managers. Industrial and Commercial Techniques.*

60. K. Polanyi, *The Great Transformation* (New York: Beacon Press, 1951).

61. J. Boddewyn, *Comparative Management and Marketing* (Glenview, Ill.: Scott, Foresman, 1969) p. 42.

62. L. Kriesberg, 'Occupational Controls among Steel Distributors', *American Journal of Sociology* (Nov 1955).

63. See L. E. Gill and L. W. Stern, 'Role and Role Theory in Distribution Channels Systems', in *Distribution Channels, Behavioral Dimensions,* ed. Stern (Boston: Houghton Mifflin, 1969) p. 28.

64. See R. K. Merton, 'The Role Set; Problems in Sociological Theory', *British Journal of Sociology,* vol. 8 (1957).

65. V. F. Ridgway, 'Administration of Manufacturer–Dealer Systems', *Administrative Science Quarterly* (Mar 1957).

66. See W. M. Evan, 'Towards a Theory of Inter-organisational Relations', *Management Science,* series B (Aug 1965).

67. Ibid.

68. J. C. Palamountain, *The Politics of Distribution* (Harvard University Press, 1955).

69. See L. W. Stern and R. H. Gorman, 'Conflict in Distribution Channels', in *Distribution Channels, Behavioral Dimensions.*

70. I. F. Wilkinson, 'Distribution Channel Management', *International Journal of Physical Distribution,* no. 1 (1973).

71. L. P. Bucklin, 'A Theory of Channel Control', *Journal of Marketing* (Jan 1973).

72. El-Ansary and Robicheaux, 'A Theory of Channel Control Revisited', *Journal of Marketing* (Jan 1974) pp. 2–7.

73. W. J. Wittreich, 'Misunderstanding the Retailer', *Harvard Business Review* (May–June 1962).

74. Galbraith and Holton, *Marketing Efficiency in Puerto Rico.*

75. See L. G. Erickson, 'Analysing Brazilian Consumer Markets', *Business Topics* (Summer 1963).

76. See D. Carson, *International Marketing: a Comparative Approach* (New York: Wiley, 1967).

77. See J. R. Grabner and L. J. Rosenberg, 'Communication in Distribution Channel Systems', in *Distribution Channels, Behavioral Dimensions.*

78. See A. Nove, *The Soviet Economy* (London: Allen & Unwin, 1969).

79. See V. I. Gogol, 'Wholesaling in the USSR', in *Comparative Marketing,* ed. Bartels (Homewood, Ill.: Irwin, 1963).

80. *Distribution of Consumer Goods.*

81. Kriesberg, 'Occupational Controls among Steel Distributors'.

172 NOTES AND REFERENCES

82. McCammon, 'Alternative Explanations of Institutional Change'.

83. Bucklin, 'The Classification of Channel Structures'.

84. T. L. Berg, 'Designing the Distribution System', in *The Social Responsibilities of Marketing*, ed. W. D. Stevens (Chicago: American Marketing Association, 1962).

85. Bierman and Dyckman, *Managerial Cost Accounting* (New York: Collier-Macmillan, 1971).

86. Dobson, *Distribution Cost Accounting* (Gee & Co., 1969).

87. A. W. Napolitan, 'Determining Optimum Distribution Points for Economical Warehousing and Transportation', in *Managing the Material Function*, A.M.A. Report No. 35 (1959).

88. A. A. Kuehn and M. J. Hamburger, 'A Heuristic Programme for Locating Warehouses', *Management Science* (July 1963) reprinted in *Marketing Logistics*, ed. N. E. Marks and R. M. Taylor (1967) pp. 91–109.

Chapter 7

1. This description follows closely that contained in Michael J. Baker, Jennifer L. Drayton and Stephen T. Parkinson, *The Adoption of New Products* (Paris: Marcel Dassault, Jours de France Foundation, 1975).

2. *Laws of Imitations* (New York: Henry Holt, 1903).

3. See, for example, Everett M. Rogers, *Diffusion of Innovations* (New York: Free Press, 1902).

4. J. K. Ryan and N. Gross, 'The Diffusion of Hybrid Seed Corn in Two Iowa Committees', *Rural Sociology*, 8 (1943).

5. J. S. Coleman, E. Katz and H. Menzel, 'The Diffusion of an Innovation among Physicians', *Sociometry*, 20 (1967).

6. Rogers, *Diffusion of Innovations*.

7. R. Lavidge and G. A. Steiner, 'A Model for Predictive Measurements of Advertising Effectiveness', *Journal of Marketing*, 25 (1961).

8. See, for example, R. Mason, 'An Ordinal Scale for Measuring the Adoption Process', in *Studies of Innovation and of Communication to the Public*, ed. Wilbur Schramm (Stanford University Institute for Communication Research, 1962); also K. S. Polda, 'The Hypothesis of a Hierarchy of Effects: A Partial Evaluation', *Journal of Marketing Research*, 3 (1966).

9. T. S. Robertson, *Innovative Behavior and Communication* (New York: Holt, Rhinehart & Winston, 1971); A. R. Andreasen, 'Attitudes and Consumer Behavior: A Decision Model', in *New Research*

in Marketing, ed. Lee E. Preston (Institute of Business and Economic Research, University of California, 1965); and F. M. Nicosia, *Consumer Decision Processes* (Englewood Cliffs, N.J.: Prentice-Hall, 1966).

10. Or, alternatively, see Baker, Drayton and Parkinson, *Adoption of New Products*.

11. Michael J. Baker, *Marketing New Industrial Products* (London: Macmillan, 1975).

12. This description follows closely that of 'A Model of the New Product Adoption Process', ch. 4 in *Marketing New Industrial Products*.

Chapter 8

1. See George Schwartz (ed.), *Science in Marketing* (New York: Wiley, 1965).

2. An exception to this is William J. Stanton, *Fundamentals of Marketing*, 4th edn (New York: McGraw-Hill, 1975), and we draw heavily on this source in this section. Another source to be consulted is John M. Rathmell, *Marketing in the Service Sector* (Cambridge, Mass.: Winthrop, 1974) which contains many useful references.

3. Stanton, *Fundamentals of Marketing*.

4. Levitt, 'Marketing Myopia', *Harvard Business Review* (July–Aug 1960).

5. Philip Kotler and Sidney J. Levy, 'Broadening the Concept of Marketing', *Journal of Marketing*, vol. 33 (Jan 1969) pp. 10–15.

6. Ibid.

Chapter 9

1. This chapter draws heavily upon an article first published in *Industrial Advertising and Marketing* (Spring 1975) and thanks are extended to the editor for permission to reproduce this material.

2. Philip Kotler, *Marketing Management*, 2nd edn (Englewood Cliffs, N.J.: Prentice-Hall, 1972).

3. P. A. Samuelson, *Economics*, 4th edn (New York: McGraw-Hill, 1958).

4. Ibid. p. 21.

5. D. Meadows *et al.*, *The Limits to Growth* (London: Earth Island, 1972).
6. See his *The Waste Markers* and *The Hidden Persuaders*.
7. See her *Silent Spring* (Harmondsworth: Penguin, 1970).
8. See his *Unsafe at Any Speed*.
9. From the *Financial Times* (24 Dec 1974).

Index